# THE MAMMOTH IN THE ROOM

How Great Leaders and Their Teams Embrace
Evolutionary Truths for Outstanding Business Results

## NICOLAS POKORNY

Editing, design, distribution by Bublish
Published by Mammoth Leadership Sciences LLC

ISBN: 978-1-647048-43-3 (paperback)
ISBN: 978-1-647048-42-6 (hardcover)
ISBN: 978-1-647048-41-9 (eBook)
ISBN: 978-1-647048-44-0 (audiobook)

# Contents

Foreword . . . . . . . . . . . . . vii

Introduction . . . . . . . . . . . . xi

## Section I: On People

Overview . . . . . . . . . . . . . 3

Chapter 1: Fix Yourself First . . . . . . . . . .41

Chapter 2: Build Your Team . . . . . . . . . .59

Chapter 3: Manage Power and Fear . . . . . . . .77

Chapter 4: Lead Like You Want to Be Led . . . . . . .97

## Section II: On Strategy

Overview . . . . . . . . . . . . . 121

Chapter 5: Recognize Tomorrow's Company
Is Today's Everyday Business . . . . . . . 131

Chapter 6: Apply a Dynamic Stability
Business Framework . . . . . . . . . 149

Chapter 7: Watch Out for Evolutionary Pitfalls,
Biases, and Mismatches . . . . . . . . 169

Chapter 8: Be Political . . . . . . . . . . 191

## Section III: On Implementation

Overview . . . . . . . . . . . . . . . . 205

Chapter 9: A Culture of Implementation Excellence. . . . 209

Chapter 10: The Hard Facts of Implementation . . . . . 215

Chapter 11: Implementation Soft Skills. . . . . . . . 225

Conclusion . . . . . . . . . . . . . . . 231

Acknowledgments . . . . . . . . . . . . . 235

About the Author . . . . . . . . . . . . . 241

Endnotes . . . . . . . . . . . . . . . . 243

*For Isabelle, Valerie, Elisa, Rafael, and Madeleine.*

# Foreword

Look at the lifespan of the five hundred biggest companies quoted on the stock exchange. It has decreased to less than twenty years. There are many reasons stated, such as insolvency, acquisitions and mergers, and asset stripping. But is there another reason behind those obvious reasons?

Rasmus Hougaard, founder and CEO of the Potential Project, which analyzes thirty-five thousand managers, reported that 65 percent of all employees wish that their boss would get fired. Eighty-two percent of all employees do not feel motivated by their managers. But 77 percent of those managers think that they do motivate their employees. So, one can conclude that a substantial, maybe overwhelming, number of employees only bring their bodies to the workplace and leave their hearts at home due to unsatisfactory leadership behavior. A Gallup research study states that 75 percent of all self-terminations are based on the behavior of the employee's managers. In 2014, in Germany alone, the costs related to absenteeism due to low emotional binding to the company amounted to 15.4 billion dollars.

These facts make it pretty clear. Leadership capabilities are the primary but most elusive elements responsible for the prosperity or the failure of a company. And they are often behind the curtain, as a mammoth in the room.

This conclusion brings us to the question of how to deal with it in terms of leadership behavior, style of leadership, and concept of leadership. In my experience as a leader and an employee, one can find companies or teams on four different levels. The lowest and most nonproductive level you can call the flight-or-fight level. This level appears often when restructuring a company, when new managers are onboarded, or when the number of employees is reduced. Typical symptoms for this level are constant quarrel and arguing, high fluctuation (mainly among the best), aggressive fights for positions, clique formations, and unproductive teamwork. When a leader can build trust and establish a constructive conflict culture, it is possible to overcome this level. In order to get there, a leader needs to enable people to talk to one another, to demonstrate deep humanity, to listen, and to ask the right questions.

With this and more, a team or company might reach the second level, the competitive level, which is where most companies are. On this level, competition and competitors get more into the focus. But on this level, it still happens that colleagues might solely be seen as competitors. In these situations, the leader has to step in, explain their values and principles, and tell those individuals that their behavior is destructive and unwanted. Additionally, a leader needs to create an environment of purpose, an atmosphere of enthusiasm, and the necessary structure and methods to keep these inspirations alive.

If a leader can master these challenges, there is a good chance of getting to the third level, the creative level. On this level, constructive collaboration in the interest of the organization visibly exists. Colleagues support one another, they share ideas, and meetings are vital, powerful, and fertile. Fluctuation and sickness ratios decline significantly. The leader must be the enabler of creativity, must create free space but simultaneously maintain a certain level of constructive tension to ensure performance on the highest aspirational level. The leader must communicate with the highest level of clarity.

After this long and challenging leadership journey, a team might reach the fourth level, what I call the flow level, which is the level of high-performance teams. On this level, teams have their vision internalized; they live their team philosophy. There is no loss of energy due to political agitation; everybody performs for the greater good and is orientated to achieve maximal success. Structure and strategies are distinct and clear. Every team member in high-performance teams is a role model for all other team members. Everything is focused on success. The flow means that success is causative for success. Enthusiasm is not only a feature within the team but also recognized by others, even by competitors.

As you can imagine, it is a journey with many challenges, barriers, and obstacles to lead a team up to the highest level. And it needs sometimes just diminutiveness to fall down to the lowest level. Years ago, I was lucky that a great leader let me take part in a journey like this, when Nicolas Pokorny became my manager. I had the big pleasure to step up to this flow level because of the leadership capabilities of this great leader, bearing so many learnings for my further career. *The Mammoth in the Room* is a logical consequence of Nicolas's capabilities, his high level of self-reflection, and his deepest interest in the well-being of people, which is the fundament of everything. To be honest, I have to say that he took too much time to write this masterpiece, as the world of leaders needed it much earlier.

**Anton M. Luchner**
Author, keynote speaker, sales trainer
General Manager of Medperion and former General Manager of Sobi Pharmaceuticals

# Introduction

Have you ever thought about how our ancestors hunted mammoths? It might seem like an odd question to open a business book, but bear with me. Here's how I think mammoth hunting might have gone down back in the day.

"Daddy, I'm hungry," one of my kids might have moaned after a long day.

"Yes. I understand. I'm sorry." I would slump to the front entrance of our family cave and observe the herd of giant woolly mammoths grazing below in the valley. *Just one of those would feed us for months! But how can I bring down such a huge, fierce beast alone?*

*Ugh*, I would think to myself, *Maybe I can work with my neighbors. They must be hungry too. But can I trust them to pull their weight during the hunt and not run off with more than their fair share after? Hmmm. I'm not sure, but I'm too hungry to care. I'll have to take that risk.*

I'd knock on the cave next door because last year my family had helped them find water in the heat of summer. Hopefully, they'd be willing to return the favor now.

"Hi. It's Nicolas. Are you guys hungry?"

"Yes!" My neighbors would nod.

"Do you want to hunt the woolly mammoth together and share it?"

"Let's do it!"

And so was born the first implementation team—tens of thousands of years before the word *company* ever existed.

What came next? We asked three more neighbors and put together our plan. Without equipment or natural speed, our small group of humans had to get creative.

"What if we dig a big pit around the corner in that valley and cover it with leaves?" one group member suggested.

Everyone started to get excited. "Yeah! We could rub some sticks together and chase them into the valley with fire."

"And use our spears to finish off the job once they fall in the covered pit."

With renewed hope and confidence, we all patted one another on the back. "Great plan! What could go wrong?"

We started digging the hole, but the soil was way harder than expected so it took us three times as long and we had to find more people to help. After the hole was finally deep enough, we camouflaged it and got ready to start our hunt. Wouldn't you know it, a big storm rolled in, and we had to abandon our fire sticks and chase the huge mammoths with our spears in the pouring rain. We yelled at the top of our lungs, trying to sound bigger and fiercer than we were. Our lives depended on catching just one mammoth, so we were fearless!

Luckily, no one slipped in the mud, got trampled, or fell into the pit. Despite the odds, we captured a woolly mammoth and achieved our goal. The rest, as they say, is history!

What does this have to do with modern business leadership? *Everything!*

We might not live in caves or chase our meals today, but we do have mouths to feed, bills to pay, families to raise, personal goals to achieve, and a life outside of work that brings us joy when we have time for it. We work together because tens of thousands of years ago, we brought down our first woolly mammoth as a unit and learned as a species that working in groups allowed us to be more successful at getting what we needed for ourselves and our families to survive and thrive. Over time, with more group successes, evolution wired this behavior into our brains. To this day, our human DNA tells us that our ability to survive and thrive as individuals is improved when we work together in groups—and so we do.

But there is one very significant difference between the past and the present.

When a group of cave dwellers brought down a mammoth, the spoils were divided fairly evenly, and the correlation between effort and individual benefit was very clear. There were no layers of bureaucracy or large multinational groups equipped with whiteboards and spreadsheets. Could you imagine some of the business units you know getting together to hunt a mammoth? There would be study groups and strategy sessions. The idea would be shopped to the right stakeholders for support. There would be time, budget, and ROI analyses across multiple departments. Let's be honest, your team would likely starve before getting close to a single woolly mammoth! You know I'm right. Still, some modern teams get the job done. They are the exception, but they exist. What makes them different? How do these teams accomplish so much while most accomplish so little?

Successful teams are led by individuals who recognize the mammoth in the room. They acknowledge and respect their people's evolutionary wiring. But no *one trains leaders how to manage the mammoth in the room, so successful leaders are scarce. Meanwhile, all that evolutionary wiring that worked so well back in ancient times is wreaking havoc on modern group dynamics at the office. It's a huge gap in our leadership training—one that most of us don't even know exists.*

*I'd like to eliminate that gap.*

With more than thirty-five years of professional experience, I have held almost every type of leadership position there is. I've led large and small teams at local companies and at multinationals. I've led from headquarters and out in the field. I have held strategy leadership roles and implementation leadership roles. I've even owned my own business. As I was thrown into each new type of leadership position, I was forced to look at myself in the mirror, reflect honestly about what I saw, and enter a state of continuous learning. In my quest to improve, I devoured books and attended seminars, lectures, and conferences. I even added a couple of university degrees. But at a certain point, I realized leadership was much simpler than it was made out to be. I discovered the mammoth in the room—and it changed everything.

Our evolutionary wiring and development are the foundation of human individual behavior and our behaviors in groups. Study this and become expert in current evolutionary theory and you'll be a better leader. Teach your people about this and you'll build teams that are unstoppable. But evolution's role in the workplace isn't a topic you'll study at business school or find in popular business books. I wrote this book to bridge a significant knowledge gap and provide emerging and senior leaders with a practical road map to become better leaders by acknowledging, respecting, and learning to deal with the mammoth in the room. How will we tackle this beast? In three different sections:

- **On People**: Leading a business is not actually about leading a business; it's about leading the people who *do* the business—and based on everything I've written so far, you know that means learning about the mammoth in the room.

- **On Strategy**: If you ask five people what strategy means, you'll get ten different answers. You're probably laughing, but it's true, right? For me, strategy is simply understanding that tomorrow's company is today's everyday business. This is the foundation of my simple Dynamic Stability Framework, which will teach you to build a culture of continuous transformation, where the mammoth in the room is always recognized and appreciated. Because who leads all transformation? People.

- **On Implementation**: This is when the rubber hits the road and you and your team go after the mammoth. Only when everything is at stake can you show the world what you're truly made of as a leader. And this comes back to your people and your ability to build a culture of implementation excellence.

To become a high-performance leader and bring about real change, you must commit to the personal and professional work required to recognize the mammoth in yourself and the room—and learn how to tame it. You must face the good, bad, and the ugly—and evolve.

# Section I

---

# On People

*A leader is best when people barely know he exists, when his work is done, his aim fulfilled, they will say: we did it ourselves.*

*—Lao Tzu*[1]

# Overview

The new CEO at Indemnify, a leading European insurance company, wanted to kick off his tenure with a bold initiative. Facing growing competition, he knew revenue growth would be tough in the coming years. New accounts would be more difficult and costly to acquire. He called in his executive team and gathered a group of expensive, top-name consultants to give him advice and ideas. After two months of meetings at headquarters (HQ), a plan was hatched. The company's successful international sales teams would be trained to compel Indemnify's existing customers to spend more money, thus helping the company overcome its revenue-growth challenge.

The initiative would require the international insurance agents and managers in twenty European countries to change the way they conducted business. Instead of meeting with clients several times a year according to individual common sense–based target plans aligned within every single sales team to maintain and build upon their relationships, the sales teams would now need to plan their customer interactions according to a strict methodology dictated by HQ. The new call plans derived from that very methodology were then supposed to be uploaded onto the newly developed, multimillion-dollar CRM (customer relation management) system, which was paid by and housed at HQ level. The insurance agents would then document each customer visit in this very CRM on their company computer and upload their work every day. This would give HQ the opportunity to follow the business (very) hands-on, on a day-by-day basis. To ensure that HQ's plans were rolled out effectively, dozens of new department leads were brought in, with a revised set of intricate key performance indicators (KPIs) to measure success according to HQ's standards. Each sales team's manager would be taken away from their regions (and accounts) and flown to HQ for a week of training on the new systems and procedures. With around two thousand insurance agents scattered across Europe, it was a big—and expensive—undertaking. All in all, the new initiative would cost Indemnify $20 million, a number that did not include the opportunity costs of decreased customer-facing activities due to trainings. No matter, it was a just the sort of big initiative the CEO needed—complete with all the bells and whistles.

It was January when the initiative kicked off, and a team of executives and consultants sat anxiously awaiting the first data at HQ. Information did indeed start rolling in, but it didn't show what they were expecting. Instead of documenting customer meetings every day and following the new sales script, the reps were reporting back maybe only once or twice a week and were entering notes rather casually, if at all. It looked like business as usual. At first, management accepted the imperfect data because everything was new. They understood the insurance agents would need some time to get fully up to speed. But even after a few months, it was more of the same. The new international sales department heads came under scrutiny, and performance pressure increased. They were told to provide assurances that the data would improve.

More HQ brainstorming led to a new incentive system that would pay insurance agents to input the right information into the CRM in the right way. Additionally, all twenty international insurance agent teams would compete for monetary incentives, and their managers would compete for career boosting awards. Almost overnight, things turned around, and HQ started to see the information they needed to support their strategy. Luckily, over the course of the initiative's eighteen-month rollout phase, revenue kept rising, as it had for the five years prior to the new initiative. The revenue crisis seemed to have been averted, and the numbers were good enough for HQ to meet their targets and declare the initiative a victory.

But was it a real victory?

A year after the roll out, HQ sent out an anonymous employee survey to gather feedback about the initiative. It revealed the following:

- The strategy was only implemented in some parts of the organization.
- The insurance agents felt controlled, over-monitored, and mistrusted.
- Only a small number of people in the organization understood HQ's strategy.
- The data had been altered by many agents to secure monetary incentives.
- Most team leaders had pushed their insurance agents to conform to the incentive protocols to keep HQ happy, resulting in many individuals entering false information into the CRM.

Does this look like success? Not so much. Why did this initiative go off the rails? Why did Indemnify's executive team see a win when the insurance agents saw the opposite? Because culture eats strategy for breakfast—every time. Employee behavior shouldn't come from a top-down demand or monetary incentives. It needs to come from the well-informed and well-supported employees who willingly buy into and support HQ strategies. This requires not only a healthy corporate culture but a CEO and executive team who respect that culture. This was not the case at Indemnify Insurance. Leadership missed a mammoth moment, a chance to understand and address the evolutionary forces at play in the execution of this strategy.

In fact, after some months of meetings, surveys, assessments, consultants' reports, and so on to get to the bottom of it, Indemnify's project leaders proclaimed that they had identified the real problem: some of the agents didn't know how to input the data correctly. They issued a recommendation: all the insurance agents would be signed up for data management training. This assignment would be added to each individual's development plan. Finally, the project leaders stated their conclusion: this new training would give each agent the skills they needed to bolster and even advance their career by supporting HQ's future strategies. Problem solved.

Really? Aren't we back at square one?

Nothing had changed fundamentally, but at least the company's leaders could say they listened to their people, right?

"Yes, we did," they can say with confidence.

I have witnessed patterns like this many times throughout my career. You might have even seen something like this happen yourself, maybe even at your own company. These types of stories unfold at companies of all sizes, and in every industry, all the time. And that's the point. While innovative strategies are great, top-down mandates dictated by headquarters or other leadership initiatives that don't consider employees' input or solicit their buy-in have a weak foundation and are unlikely to be executed as planned. Without a healthy culture that understands and supports the company strategy, most HQ initiatives fail. This, however, doesn't stop executives from spinning things to look like a win. Not only is there too much riding on each success for company leadership to admit failure, there's also often a misguided belief that the initiative did actually work, despite plenty of evidence to the contrary. In the case of Indemnify, revenue went up, so HQ assumed the initiative drove this growth, which is a questionable conclusion based on the findings of the employee survey and the fact that revenue increased the previous years as well. It's a vicious cycle that plays out in thousands of companies around the world. Unfortunately, over time, the underlying problems continue to go unaddressed and whittle away at ongoing growth and innovation.

If you build a strategy without your culture in mind, you're doomed. Period.

It always amazes me how much time and money companies spend figuring out *what* needs to be done and how little time and money on *how* it will be done. There are strategic workshops, planning decks with hundreds of colorful slides, and hypersophisticated KPIs with related dashboards—all of which have a natural half-life equaling the tenure of the department manager who demanded their development. We use such KPIs to measure our strategy and implementation success and justify the money and time spent on all of it. We tell ourselves, "This is what our market research told us we needed to track." Then we spend millions more on consulting companies that explain what needs to be done based on that same market research. Somehow, we forget (or perhaps we were not aware) that this new consultancy is only advising us because three years ago, another manager—who has since left the company—commissioned them with a similar project. So, despite all the time, energy, and money spent on *what* needs to be done, the company has made no progress toward resolving its issues—and so, the cycle of madness continues.

In addition to all of that, leadership teams continue to tell their people, almost as an afterthought, "Focus on your people!"

As a leader, you tell yourself, "Of course, I want to focus on my people and our culture. They are central to our success. I know this!"

But still, there are all those other demands on your time. It's a bit like riding a bike while juggling several plates. Then, HQ tosses you one plate more midjourney. You catch it and keep riding, trying to stay upright and on course while juggling a growing number of plates. It's an impossible task. As a result, people, culture, and the *how* to get things get done come in the form of well-intentioned but half-baked initiatives—things like development plans to manage the workforce and drive the company's strategy and more employee surveys that reveal an underwhelmed and demotivated workforce that thinks the company has too much bureaucracy, makes too many top-down decisions, and ignores employees' attempts to have some semblance of work-life balance.

What comes after the leadership teams read these employee responses? Meetings and team-building workshops are scheduled, during which people vent their frustrations. Typically, the folks who complain the most about the company's demotivating bureaucracy end up leading a new project on how to reduce bureaucracy. Ironic, right? They've added a new task to their already full plates, making them complicit in the very problem they are supposed to be battling. The new project turns into an additional workstream, even though the ones who understand human motivation know it will not fix the problem, because the demotivating factors do not equal the motivating ones.[2] This is classic Herzberg's motivation-hygiene theory, which, if you haven't already studied it, is worth some research time and attention. As I've mentioned, companies spend 95 percent of their time on strategy, tactics, and implementation but only 5 percent on their people. This is the core problem. When a strategy succeeds (or appears to succeed), we say it's brilliant. When it fails, it is very difficult to decipher whether the strategy was wrong or whether it failed because the culture was not ready for it. How can anyone know for sure why some strategies succeed while others do not? In the case of failure, is there a chance that the company's culture was ill prepared, not fully adapted, not properly equipped, just plain toxic, or simply intolerant of the strategy? Yes, there definitely is. On the other hand, isn't there also a chance that sometimes companies get lucky that the culture tolerated its strategy, even though much more could have been achieved if the culture had been more fully involved? Couldn't an engaged culture drive success for even a mediocre strategy? How can leaders know what is driving outcomes, especially if they don't know their people or understand what drives their behaviors? In short, when they don't address the mammoth in the room. They can't.

## What Is Corporate Culture Anyway?

*Corporate culture* is a popular term these days. It is bandied about in magazine articles, in business presentations, and by executives, managers, and consultants. But what *is* culture, really? How is it built? Why does it matter? Fact is, if you ask ten people to define corporate culture, you'll get ten different answers. Here are some I find quite useful. According to a March 2018 McKinsey blog titled "Culture: 4 keys to why it matters," by Carolyn Dewar and Reed Doucette, "Culture is the common set of behaviors and underlying mindsets and beliefs that shape how people work and interact day to day."[3] In their January 2019 issue titled "The Culture Factor," *Harvard Business Review* uses different words but with a comparable meaning: "Culture is the tacit social order of an organization: It shapes attitudes and behaviors in wide-ranging and durable ways. Cultural norms define what is encouraged, discouraged, accepted, or rejected within a group."[4] Do a search for "corporate culture" and you'll find many other definitions.

The wide variety of definitions is understandable because culture is the representation of human behavior, which is difficult to define in absolute terms. To make things even more complicated, corporate culture deals with human behavior *in a group setting*—small groups of individual employees, larger department-level groups, subsidiary and affiliate groups with hundreds of members, and even global groups with thousands of participants. The largest corporate cultures comprise groups in the hundreds of thousands, spread across the world like the diaspora of a small country. There are groups upon groups, and there are groups that manage groups. We've all experienced this.

No matter what size the company, culture represents how people interact with one another, what they believe in, what they accept or do not accept—alone and in groups. And what I know for sure is that culture is a key factor in defining a company's destiny—for better or for worse. Yet, we watch CEOs on quarterly earnings calls talk about absolutely everything—new products, building the perfect prospect pipeline, increasing structural investments, their competitors' strategies, and so on—while only rarely mentioning a single cultural initiative. This persists, even though it is now widely accepted that culture has a monumental impact on a CEO's ultimate success or failure. The 2018 McKinsey blog referenced above said it best:

1.  Culture correlates with performance. Based on our research of over 1,000 organizations those with top quartile cultures (as measured by our Organizational Health Index) post a return to shareholders 60 percent higher than median companies and 200 percent higher than those in the bottom quartile.

2.  Culture is inherently difficult to copy. The quickening pace of innovation means that products and business models face the constant threat of being replicated. In this environment, the ultimate competitive advantage is a healthy culture that adapts automatically to changing conditions to find new ways to succeed.

3.  Healthy cultures enable organizations to adapt. In a world where the one constant is change, culture becomes even more important because organizations with high-performing cultures thrive on change while unhealthy cultures have above 50 percent chance of failure in times of transformation.

4. Unhealthy cultures lead to underperformance . . . or worse. Over time, not only do unhealthy cultures foster lackluster performance, but they can also bring companies down.

Culture is so important, which is why we pay it so much lip service. But we don't walk the talk. We spend days, weeks, even months preparing next year's strategic goals but devote hardly any time to building a strong culture to support our strategic goals. Isn't that counterintuitive? Shouldn't we be spending more time on the people and culture that must execute on these initiatives? Shouldn't that be part of the strategy? Without a more balanced approach, it feels a bit like we are talking about a wonderful place we want to reach without thinking about how we're going to get there. We somehow assume that a healthy culture will just emerge, or that it's already there, or that we'll just adapt and grow a culture along the way. Without a road map to prepare our people to help us reach our destination, we get lost and never actually arrive. This is the unfortunate narrative at many companies. There's too much "stuff" to do around hunting down the next KPI or solving the next crisis. Most companies never move beyond this reactive state, so they never get ahead of the game. Sadly, the leaders at these companies never find time to make culture a focus.

**Why Culture Matters**

According to economics professor and lecturer Dr. Peter Herbek of Danube University in Krems, Austria, the elements of corporate cultures that produce the 2018 McKinsey sourced four keys as to what makes culture matter to employees are outlined below. The corporate culture must be:

1. **Implicit.** Common attitudes and behavioral patterns are implicit. They are not conceived but lived.

2. **Collective.** Determined by common orientations and standardized patterns of action for all members.

3. **Interpretive.** Common interpretations in a complex world offer security and orientation.

4. **Emotional.** They should shape the emotional life of the system by standardizing what is loved or liked—and what is disliked or hated.

5. **Historical.** They result from historical learning processes. This collective store of knowledge reflects the development of the company.

6. **Interactive.** It is not the documented leadership principles that cultivate culture but the actual behaviors of the culture's leaders. Corporate cultures are passed on through interaction and cannot be learned consciously.

Another reason culture gets left off the agenda so often is because it's difficult to quantify the short-term results of a strengthened culture. Despite research indicating that 91 percent of managers in the US say a job candidate's alignment with a company's culture is equal to or more important than his or her skills and experience,[5] it can be challenging to build a business case for culture. Though a change in culture can lead to profound, positive outcomes over time, those outcomes are not always tangible or measurable, especially in the beginning. Improvements in performance, strategy, outcomes, and innovation may be everywhere, but the correlation to an improved culture can be hard to demonstrate. Working on corporate culture cannot be a project, a program, a biannual survey, or a yearly team-building effort. It must be a unified, continuous focus—a commitment, a pledge—by everyone in the organization.[6] Once this pledge is acknowledged and leaders in an organization are given the green light to prioritize culture—and given the necessary background on human behavior—there is a good chance they can finally move the needle in the right direction. But how do we set this in motion? How do we get this important conversation started?

## Human Behavior: An Evolutionary Perspective [7] [8] [9]

Have you ever asked yourself why the behavior of leading and following others even developed? What it is for? Leadership and followership evolved in humans (and in other species) to solve recurrent coordination problems. Basically, leadership can be defined as coordination of two or more individuals to accomplish joint goals.[10] [11] What was the problem to be solved for us humans? Movement! Social species—like us—stay alive by moving together. But when do you move, where, who moves first, and who follows? Hence, the classic coordination problem that gave rise to the emergence of leadership is group movement, and it can be solved by some individuals seizing the initiative to lead and others to follow.[12]

What does that have to do with business leadership, you might ask? Well, in business leadership, we are coordinating ourselves toward certain goals—business goals in our case. Therefore, we need to acknowledge two things: first, that leading a business means leading the people who actually do the business; second, that leading people in a corporate setting means steering individual human behavior in groups. This means we must encourage individuals to align their priorities so we can all move in the same direction. To do this, we need to first understand a bit more about human behavior—both as individuals and individuals in groups.

Let me share what I have learned in my thirty-plus years of leading people. It has been a most challenging, gratifying, and humbling journey—and a true honor. What all these years of learning, stumbling, and growing as a leader have taught me is immeasurable. My career has taken me around the globe to live and work in many different countries, markets, and cultures. I have logged literally millions of travel miles. I have held many different leadership roles at the local, regional, and global level. These leadership experiences also came in all sizes—from one person reporting to me to several hundred through multiple management levels. They also came in various structures, from units to matrices to project groups—you name it, I've probably led it.

I found my first experiences leading just a few people to be exhausting, time-consuming, and perplexing. Human behavior was often incomprehensible to me. I felt frustrated, even angry sometimes. Some attitudes and actions I encountered kept me up at night. I'd ask myself, "Why on earth do they not understand the best thing to do in this situation?" or "Why are they acting this way?" or "Why are these people not championing my amazing plan?"

Does this sound familiar?

As I mentioned earlier, a company's culture—whether large or small—is shaped by human behavior. But as leaders, the behavior of colleagues can sometimes seem irrational. What are they thinking? Such feelings and reactions are common and completely understandable. Think about it—you're asked as a leader to contribute to shaping your company's culture, but no one gives you any training on the human behavior that drives that culture. Nor do they help you address the mammoth looming in every professional interaction, collaboration, meeting, and boardroom. You're taught how create business plans, strategies, P&Ls, presentations, and so forth, but no one teaches you a thing about human behavior—despite the fact that you have real humans reporting to you every day. This seems like a big gap in your education, doesn't it? I agree. And that is why I'd like to start filling that gap by revisiting the theories of Charles Darwin, *the renowned British naturalist, geologist, biologist, and father of evolutionary theory*—but with a business lens.

### How Behavior Develops

Every behavior has a *how* (as in how it works) and a *why* (as in why it exists). This *how* and *why* are rooted in our evolution. As scientists have demonstrated, all animal behaviors, including ours as humans, can be characterized by proximate and ultimate sequences (Alcock, 1996). Proximate sequences represent our genome's interaction with the environment, leading to the formation of human sensory and motor structures during our ontogenesis. For instance, our nervous system has developed to perceive stimuli from the environment, our hormone system for regulating our internal responsiveness to these stimuli, and our musculoskeletal system to run the necessary behavioral responses. Ultimate sequences, on the other hand, represent the evolutionary origins and modifications of our behaviors over time. For example, ultimate sequences describe how past natural selection and reproductive successes have shaped our present behaviors (Tinbergen, 1963; Sherman, 1988). In other words, proximate sequences reveal *how* a behavior developed, and ultimate sequences tell us *why* they developed.

Let's look at an example of proximate and ultimate sequences to which most of us can all relate. Do you like to indulge in a slice of cake or piece candy occasionally? Of course! Have you ever asked yourself why? Well, the *how*, or the proximate sequence, reveals that our biological system links the intake of certain sugar-like molecular structures to the pleasure center in our brains. The *why*, or the ultimate sequence, recognizes sweetness as high-calorie food source that will help us energize our bodies and survive. Both help explain human desire for all things sweet!

I like this particular example because today, overconsumption represents a huge health threat to industrialized societies. Overconsumption of sweets and other high-calorie, low-nutrition-value foods has contributed to an epidemic of obesity that comes with many health problems, including diabetes and heart disease. Health statistics show that in industrialized societies, people eat more than they need. While we are not able to ignore our preference for sweets from a behavioral perspective, modern science has found a way to trick the human brain with low-calorie artificial sweeteners that satisfy the pleasure center of the brain without ingesting too many calories—at least this is how it works in theory.

## Darwin's Theory of Natural Selection

We've all heard of and studied at one point in our education Charles Darwin's theories of natural selection, first published in 1859 in his famous book, *On the Origin of Species*.[13] But there are few business schools or courses that link Darwin's theories to leadership success. That's unfortunate. As a leader, I try to keep these biological concepts front and center. It seems useless and somewhat foolish to ignore hundreds of thousands of years of evolution. Why create strategies and policies that fight how we are wired as humans? I've found it much more effective to study and respect these realities. With this in mind, I ask you to let me lead you through a quick refresher course on human evolution, with the goal of helping you more fully understand yourself and the people you are leading.

Darwin's famous phrase "survival of the fittest" has been frequently misinterpreted to mean the strongest will survive. Actually, this isn't what that phrase means at all. What Darwin was referring to was genetic fitness, not strength. Genetic fitness comes from an individual's ability to adapt successfully to its ever-changing environment and pass that adaptation on to the next generation. What Darwin was saying was that the most adaptive individual—not necessarily the strongest—will survive and thrive. Guided by this reality, the human brain has evolved over millions of years since the first hominins appeared on earth around two basic and interconnected principles:

- First and foremost, we are survival machines. We are programmed to survive, reproduce, and make sure our offspring have enough of the right resources to survive and thrive as well. That's how we pass on our genetic traits and maximize our own stake of genes within the pool of genes of the next generation. It's a big deal, and that's why self-interest shapes all of our decisions.

- Second, but equally important, our chances of surviving and thriving only exist when we collaborate with other members of our species. Have you ever looked in the mirror and asked yourself how a species as naturally slow and weak—and without natural-born weapons or shelter—has been able to conquer the planet? We have survived and thrived as a species in good part because we collaborate in every aspect of our existence and learn from that collaboration. Then, we pass it on to the next generation so they can harness this evolutionary wisdom and build upon it. We are social animals. We are wired to collaborate to ensure our individual survival and that of our offspring. We collaborate because doing so is aligned with our natural self-interest.

Without collaboration and teamwork, we would not have survived our early nomadic, hunter-gatherer times because we would not have been able to take down a mammoth singlehandedly—leaving us without food and protection. We learned collaboration was necessary. This was the foundation we needed to discover and conquer the planet. From the Neolithic Revolution, fast-forward to more recent times, to the Industrial Revolution for example, and you can see how collaboration models enabled us to mass-produce goods. Even more recently, when JFK announced that the US would put a man on the moon, he banked on the collaboration of tens of thousands of brilliant scientists to turn this vision into a reality. And in 2020, when the COVID-19 pandemic hit, international cooperation across the globe was required to preserve human life. Our early evolutionary instincts are still relevant. They still work.

**Group Selection versus Individual Selection**

Group selection is a theory of evolution that proposes that natural selection acts at the level of the group rather than at the level of the individual. It explores the idea that individuals are willing to sacrifice themselves for the greater good of the species. In absolute terms, this would mean that in situations of very scarce resources for a group of, say, ten people, one member would say, "Okay, we don't have enough food for all of us to survive, so—even though I don't know most of you—I'll sacrifice myself to make sure our species survives." Really? Individual selection, on the other hand, theorizes that in such a situation, people would try to do whatever is needed to ensure their own survival, including the genetically related individuals. Basically, they would try to survive at any costs—even killing one another. This also seems extreme. Enter Charles Darwin and his brilliant and provocative book *On the Origin of Species*, which was published on November 24, 1859. Darwin realized that among all the species he had observed, three phenomena were omnipresent:

1. **Variability.** This means that members of a species differ in their characteristic traits.

2. **Heritability.** This is the genetic act of parents passing on characteristic traits to their descendants.

3. **Differences in Reproductive Success.** Due to particular hereditary qualities in relation to current environmental conditions, some individuals leave more offspring than others.

Darwin concluded that these three phenomena program evolutionary changes. Individuals with genetic traits that enable them to establish behaviors favorable for survival within current environmental conditions reproduce more successfully than those with genetics that enable them to establish behaviors less favorable for survival within current environmental conditions. Darwin called this process *natural selection*. Darwin's masterstroke? He formulated his theory a century *before* the fundamental scientific discoveries that would support it. Today, we know that Darwin was referencing the work of nucleic acids, the building blocks of all life. We now know how Darwin's theories are carried out in human biology:

1. Variability is secured by alleles, which allow the same gene within a species to be expressed in slightly different forms. This is the foundation for a whole cascade of small differences that also interact with one another, causing additional variations of gene expression. This is what leads to the differing genetic potential of two individuals from the same species.

2. Heritability, which Darwin discussed on an individual level, can now be applied more widely to the human species, due to our understanding of how the alleles work to pass down variations from parents to offspring.

3. Differing reproductive success, we now know, occurs when some alleles are copied more often by their carriers than other alleles of the same gene. The alleles enable different traits and behaviors that create differences in reproductive success in relation to current environmental factors.

Just to be crystal clear, this science supports the widely accepted theory that humans are not formed by either genetics or environmental factors but by the interplay of both. All of this clarifies Darwin's statement about the "survival of the fittest," a statement that to this day is still often interpreted falsely because people interpret the term *fittest* as meaning *strongest*, which it does not. Darwin postulated that individuals who are able to adapt to changing environmental conditions will carry alleles that offer the best possibility of forming better adaptive behaviors relative to those conditions than other individuals of the same population, will have higher reproductive success and therefore are optimizing the stake of their own genes in the gene-pool of the next generation. What Darwin described in fitness is about success at surviving and reproducing, not about exercise and strength.

## Collaboration Is Not a Choice

The reality is that collaboration for humans is not a choice; it is a necessity for survival. To a great extent, collaboration defines us as a species. Nothing seems impossible when we can tap into the collective brainpower, spirit, and manpower of humanity. But doesn't collaboration conflict with our primal self-interests as individuals? Won't we always put our own priorities above the interests of the group? How are these seemingly opposing forces kept in balance? Specifically, how does this all work in a professional organization with hundreds, perhaps thousands, of individual employees working in groups, with a lot of the individuals in those groups striving for their next promotion or pay raise?

It's complicated, to say the least.

The Indemnify Insurance story is a perfect example of everything that can go wrong when human behavior is not aligned with a company's culture. The top-down strategies were not understood or supported by the insurance sales agents who were asked to carry them out, and the managers failed to understand the misguided human behavior they were encouraging through their incentives. And when the insurance sales agents filled out the company survey and shared what had really happened, the executive team ignored the feedback and declared victory. What a mess! This mess was created because Indemnify's leadership team either ignored, knew nothing about, or failed to reflect upon the basics of human behavior in the first place. Somebody with an understanding of human behavior would certainly not have coupled the tracking of the "right data" with monetary incentives. That's certainly ignoring the mammoth in the room, which is almost always costly.

Human behavior around collaboration continued to evolve throughout our existence as species, but it accelerated during and after the Neolithic Revolution, which is when *Homo sapiens* started to settle, divide labor, specialize, produce food, etc. This time period is considered the start of human civilization, which can be defined through the existence of following characteristics:

- Stratified political organization (public or state system).
- Economic organization with markets and trade.
- Spatial, areal organization—for example, the building of villages or towns.
- Ethical and religious beliefs.
- Transmission of tradition through written records.

If an individual is part of a political organized entity (like a state), and lives in a spatial organization (like a village), and as such is part of an economy, then the individual experiences many benefits: they are part of a social system, protected by the group, enjoy the division and specialization of labor, and so on. Though the individual must give up certain freedoms and learn to navigate the challenges of civilization, the benefits far outweigh the negatives.

The same is true for all humans in companies. Organizations provide work, a salary, health insurance, legal protection, paid vacations, maybe even a car and a cell phone. For the employees, there are numerous clear advantages and benefits to joining and staying with a company. But our brains are also trained to question the trade-offs required to receive these benefits. We're always assessing. Our brains are wired to figure out if joining or staying with a particular organization is worth the effort. It's a delicate balancing act, and we are constantly questioning everything. For example:

- Are there any downsides to working for this organization?
- Are there any strings attached to all the benefits this organization has to offer?
- Which and how many of these strings am I willing to accept in order to benefit from belonging to this organization?
- How long do I want to be a part of an organization that is struggling? Potentially, there are other organizations that are better off, where I also would be better off.
- What kind of investment or sacrifice am I prepared to make to enjoy the benefits of this organization, and will they pay off for me as an individual?

The human brain is in a never-ending assessment loop trying to figure out the delicate balance between self-interest and the needs of the group. When it comes to human behavior in corporate groups, even simple things can become complicated. For example, when a manager asks his team to embark and collaborate on an important project, each team member ponders the following two questions:

- What is the value of this task to the company?
- What is the value of this task to me as an individual?

The first question seems fairly easy for the employee to answer. Corporate goals are typically pretty straightforward. If an employee or manager meets the goals that have been defined, it is likely the impact will be positive for the organization. But what if the company is not well-run or the executive leadership team is out of touch, as was the case at Indemnify? In this case, you can bet that those insurance sales agents weighed the pros and cons of cheating by entering the data into the CRM in order to satisfy mandates from HQ and benefit from cash rewards. And guess what? Most of them ended up entering false data in order to achieve HQ's goals and get the incentives they were promised. Yet, despite this, Indemnify characterized the whole project as a win. That's some twisted thinking! In two to three years, when Indemnify starts to feel the negative impacts of not addressing its real issues or fixing its culture, those same insurance sales agents will ask themselves, "How long do I want to be a part of an organization that is struggling? Maybe I should leave." And guess who jumps ship first? The top performers. And naturally, the loss of key talent speeds up the company's decline.

The second question is more difficult for the employee to answer from the get-go. It only leads to more questions:

- How many hours will I miss with my family if I commit to this extra project?
- Will I get the appropriate credit for my work and finally get my promised promotion?
- Is there a bonus or raise involved, or just extra hours?
- Are powerful people involved in the project who could give me extra exposure to higher-ups?
- Do I respect my boss enough to put in the necessary effort?"

Basically, the famous four letters and ultimate question—WIFM or "What's in It for Me?"—is being asked by hundreds or thousands of employees around the world 24/7. With a mix of personal, professional, and group dynamics, you can see how complex this all becomes at scale. For employees, the assessment is about whether the collaboration needed to meet the organization's goals aligns with their personal and professional aspirations, all of which are driven by self-interest.

It's an assessment that employees at every level of every company make every day. And if you're in the driver's seat as a leader, this makes your life quite difficult. Keeping the answers to these two questions aligned while managing teams of people through multiple management layers can become very challenging—and the larger the team, the more complex and difficult the challenge. And never forget that your own interests drive the exact same dynamics for you as a leader. Messy, right?

Since leaders must address this alignment problem in a group setting, let's start with some principles around how groups of humans function. Remember, the biology and evolution of our species has made one thing clear: no one is wired to sacrifice themselves for the group unless their individual self-interest is somehow served.[14] [15] You might ask, "Then why do so many people do so much for others?" It's a very good question. We may be wired to make sacrifices for our families, which is an investment in our own genes, but why do we volunteer in our communities, in clubs, associations, churches, schools, and more? These benefit individuals to whom we are not related. At first blush, it might seem that we are benevolent and placing the needs of the group before our own. Nothing could be further from the truth. As we have already explored, humans have a clear self-interest in collaborating with other humans and supporting the larger community. Groups help individuals survive and thrive. Community activities bring us social status and influence, which can grow into a sort of social currency that can help us accomplish things that require the help of others. This is why we take part in the annual corporate blood drive, donate gifts to the homeless shelter at the company holiday party, and so forth. These human behavioral patterns developed and got perfected over the course of our evolution so that they are ingrained in our culture, so that our central nervous system's biochemical transmitter environment can us feel good when we help others and can make us feel guilty when we don't.[16]

### The Mass Suicide of Lemmings

Despite Charles Darwin's profound contributions, questions about the purpose of evolutionary adaptation remain. Does evolution exist to achieve higher reproductive success determined by the fact that individuals seek to maximize their fitness? Or does evolution exist to ensure the survival of as many individuals with similar genetics as possible, which in turn ensures the survival of a species?

One of the most famous works of research exploring these questions was called, *Animal Dispersion in Relation to Social Behavior* by V. C. Wynne-Edwards, published in 1962. The study examined the interest of species that use vital resources so sparingly that the whole population can consistently exist. This meant that species that kept their population density low would have a better chance of surviving at the species level. Species without such control mechanisms would have trouble competing. The research implied that individuals of a successful species might sacrifice themselves if necessary for the benefit of the species. These findings seemed logical, were widely accepted, and were supported and taught by many famous scientists at that time. The research of the three founders of ethology—Konrad Lorenz, Karl von Frisch, and Niko Tinbergen, who were awarded the 1973 Nobel Prize in Medicine—was mostly based on this assumption. The theory was also quite comforting to many. Theologians and philosophers felt it returned some humanity to evolutionary theory—that is, it hinted at mankind's evolution toward sacrifice, helpfulness, and unselfishness. As nice as the theory of group selection sounded to everyone, it just didn't hold water. In 1966, a researcher named G.C. Williams proved convincingly that Wynne-Edwards's research was wrong—and he did so with the help of a very interesting species: mountain lemmings (*Lemmus lemmus*), a remarkable species I remember studying when I was a schoolkid. Apparently, mountain lemmings commit suicide whenever the food resources of a local population are too scarce to feed all its members. This behavior seemed to align perfectly with Wynne-Edwards's theory. Mountain lemmings sacrificed themselves for the benefit of their species. I still remember wondering as a ten-year-old student, *How the heck do they choose who needs to go?*

G.C. Williams raised the following concern with the theory: even if we assume these animals do commit suicide, natural selection based on genetics within this population would still take place. This "ability" to commit suicide would be part of the mix. Thus, by definition, individuals are pre-programmed with different genetics. This is verifiable biochemically and in terms of probability—mathematically predictable and provable. Putting this into action for our mountain lemmings, this means that if some of their population's genetic code encouraged "early suicide" based on some type of environmental trigger like shortage of food, these suicides would ensure that the group of "less suicidal" lemmings would have a greater reproductive success based on their longer lifespan. In other words, they would have more time and thus more opportunities to breed than the "early suicide" group. As a result, the "less suicidal" genetic pool would increase in the lemming population and the "early suicide" genetic pool would decrease. This would continue generation after generation until eventually, only lemmings with "no appetite for suicide" would remain and the "early suicide" gene would disappear. With this train of thought, Williams proved that before selection at the species level can take place within a population, selection at the individual level would ensure that only individuals can successfully reproduce themselves over time. Thus, the process of natural selection that tackles the differences between individuals has a stronger influence on the genetic pool of the next generation than the selection based on differences between groups.

Society and communities within societies reward "team players" and are annoyed by those who benefit from the group's goodwill without contributing to it. Why? Because the team players bring the individuals in a group closer, making the group more effective. Selfish individuals can tear apart even tightly knitted groups, making the group less effective. And since we need effective group collaboration to survive and thrive as individuals, the team players serve our self-interest.

I know it's tricky, but is it starting to make sense now?

Since these are the drivers for human behavior in group dynamics, the question becomes: What are the mechanisms by which leaders can successfully navigate the delicate dance between these two forces—self-interest and the need for collaboration—and foster a high-performing group? Perhaps the easiest way to explain this concept is to start with a ridiculous, hypothetical situation that would never happen. Bear with me, I am exaggerating to make an important point.

> One day, your boss marches into your office and says, "Hello, I have some amazing news to share. You know how I admire your work. I was planning to promote you to a fabulous new leadership position that I've created within our organization. You are completely qualified for the job and your commitment to this company makes you the right person. However, I'm going to give the job to Sam from the sales team because you've already had two promotions in the last eighteen months and it just wouldn't be fair to give you another promotion so quickly, even though you've earned it. Yes, you're a better fit based on your competencies and skills, but we must be fair for the sake of the team and our public image. I know you'll be reporting to Sam from here on out and he'll be making more money than you, but you're such a nice person and such a team player that I'm sure you'll work things out for the greater good, right? Your turn will come. Are you on board?"

The story sounds outrageous, right? No leader in their right mind would go into an employee's office and explicitly lay out such a scenario—would they? No, not explicitly, but implicitly, this happens every day. Maybe the stories are not as dramatic as the one above, but I assure you, leaders—even good ones—constantly assume that their people are willing to sacrifice their own needs and desires in order to support their team and company. Such an approach goes against our wiring, our human biology, yet the assumption is commonplace. Leaders need to understand that the individual will always come first! Leaders need to understand that collaboration only exists because it supports individual survival and well-being. But because most leaders either have little or no basic understanding of the background of human behavior, these facts are often ignored or overlooked. People don't rise through the ranks at a company because they understand or apply their knowledge about human behavior. They are promoted because they achieved something or were very good at something. Maybe they had the highest sales. Maybe they had increased revenue growth. Maybe they led a "successful" project or produced the most successful marketing campaign. The list goes on. But can you remember a time when the boss said, "Congratulations! We've noticed that you have an excellent understanding of human behavior through which you will be able to merge the individual goals of your employees with the company's goals." I'm betting you can't, right? Even though this is exactly what companies should be looking for when they promote someone into a leadership position. How can anyone lead humans without understanding human behavior? It seems like such a basic requirement, but it's almost never considered.

It's time for leaders to respect the fact that self-interest—not benevolence—is what drives people to excel both as individuals and in groups. Leaders who are willing to accept that the needs of the individual shape the behavior of the group possess a powerful tool—one that can help them harness and maximize the power of both. If you'd like to see what that looks like, just consider all our species has achieved during our short time here on planet Earth. When you lead a team, you must have this biological construct in your mind.

Of course, people sometimes feel uncomfortable, even guilty, about the idea that everything we do as humans is driven by self-interest. As a result, there's a lot of denial going on. We tell ourselves, "I gave at our company's blood drive because the community needed blood. I wanted to help my fellow humans." We proudly wear our "I Gave Blood" T-shirt at the office. We feel great. But what about the people who get paid $200 to give plasma? Why don't we see those people wearing T-shirts that say "I Gave Blood and Received $200 for It"?

Because the group had to pay for these people to participate. As a result, these individuals are not thought of as benevolent team players. They were incentivized to support the larger good. Those who give to the group seemingly without repayment are celebrated, despite the fact that they have earned reciprocal social currency that is probably of much higher value than the $200 paid to the plasma donors. Society might not see the equation this way, but it's a perspective worth considering.

There is nothing wrong with being paid to give plasma. *Self-interest is not selfishness.* In fact, self-interest is essential for happiness and well-being. It creates a healthy balance between the priorities of the individual and those of the group. Selfishness is destructive. Selfish individuals don't care about being team players. From an evolutionary perspective, our behavior must align with our self-interest. But from the same evolutionary standpoint, selfishness is *against* the group and potentially sets up the group and all the individuals in the group for failure. While self-interest ensures we never take more from the group than we're prepared to give, selfishness goes against our self-interest by undermining the power of the group to improve our chances to survive and thrive as individuals.

There is an entire cultural mythology that has evolved around heroizing those who put the group before themselves. These individuals are portrayed in movies, books, and music as heroes, as "selfless"—literally defined as having no concern for oneself—even though our genetic wiring makes this virtually impossible. Think of any disaster movie you've seen in which the main character risks his or her life to save their town. Superheroes are almost always characterized as selfless. They have no concern for their personal safety. They are willing to sacrifice their lives to keep the world safe. We love this myth. We like to think of ourselves as that kind of person because we are uncomfortable with the notion of our own self-interest.

We've all heard leaders say, "Do what's best for the company!" or "Put your own interests after the team's!" Maybe you've even said these things yourself as a leader. Big mistake. All too often, leaders assume team members are "selfless" because these leaders don't understand the underlying drivers of human behavior. In reality, teams are only effective if the needs of the individuals on the team are respected. If individual boundaries are not respected or team members are not recognized for their unique capabilities, contributions, and performance, things will go south for the whole team. Some individuals are likely to leave. The departure of talented individuals then negatively impacts the entire team, especially if those individuals are top performers. While leaders need their teams to achieve the company's goals, they can't just think "team first." This approach defies human evolution and puts the team's performance and the company's strategic goals at risk. It should be "individual first," because only that allows leaders to build strong teams. Ironically, leaders are sometimes criticized for focusing too much on individuals and not enough on the team. The reasons cited are:

- Teams can achieve much more than individuals.
- Research shows that great teams have members who share goals, have one another's back, deprioritize their own interests, share resources willingly, and focus on the collective success.
- Research also shows that nonfunctioning teams have members who focus on their own interests, compete with others for resources, live and perform by their own standards, and focus first and foremost on their own success.

The message of this research is clear. However, it explores outcomes, not how we arrived at those outcomes. Unfortunately, these outcomes are then put on a spec sheet for leadership workshops and seminars and the attendees are then told to "behave" like that. The entry fee to join a team is to put your individuality aside because individual ambition is not a real thing. Then, we are a great team! Unfortunately, this encourages leaders to tell their people not to think about their individual interests. But human evolution and thus human behavior do not work that way. Once again, the mammoth in the room is dismissed at leadership's peril, and the dysfunction continues. Conversely, top-performing teams—where everyone understands the group's greater purpose, shares the same team goals, helps and supports one another, shares resources, and collaboration is king—are built *around* the individuality of the group's members. They work because the leader understands that healthy team dynamics require that the individuals on that team are fostered first. Leaders who run these types of successful teams encourage members to live their individuality. They recognize and appreciate that the individuals on their team are striving toward their own goals along with the team's goals. They recognize the mammoth in the room and respect the healthy interplay between self-interest and group dynamics. Companies and departments with these types of leaders, teams, and cultures almost always outperform their competitors. The best leaders are able to show their people how a successful, collaborative team can align around common goals while maintaining healthy self-interest as individuals. When you master the skills necessary to build a culture where individuals are respected and have the ability to grow, develop, and contribute to the group for their *own* good, your company's performance will improve dramatically. To be a successful leader capable of driving strong performance, you must master this challenging balancing act between team and individual success—even in the face of criticism.

## Game Theory[17] [18]

Sometimes, when the biological aspects of human behavior are discussed, you hear people saying, "That's not applicable to us anymore because we have evolved beyond our early human biology."

Are there models that prove that underlying evolutionary factors still drive human behavior in today's modern society? Yes, there are. Game theory is a perfect example. Game theory is a fascinating and powerful framework for understanding how individuals, firms, and even nations make strategic decisions in a wide range of contexts, as described by Dr. Ritikesh Kumar, lecturer at the Department of Mathematics at the Government Girls College in Gurugram, Haryana, India. It is a theoretical framework for conceiving social scenarios among competing players. So, in some respects, game theory is the science of strategy, or at least of the optimal decision-making of independent and competing actors in a strategic setting.[19] "It offers insights into the intricate interplay of choices, outcomes, and rationality, making it a valuable tool in fields as diverse as economics, political science, biology, and psychology. This groundbreaking treatise revolutionized the study of strategic interactions, introducing the world to concepts that continue to shape our understanding of decision-making."[20] Mathematician John von Neumann and economist Oskar Morgenstern did the pioneering work to establish the field in the first half of the twentieth century and laid its foundation in their seminal work *Theory of Games and Economic Behavior*.[21] One other person, however, literally changed the game of game theory—the mathematician John F. Nash, who attended Carnegie Institute of Technology and then afterward moved to Princeton University, where he began working on his equilibrium theory for which he also received the 1994 Nobel Prize for Economics.[22] Later, he joined MIT as faculty member. His research led to great advancements in the field and extended the analysis beyond zero-sum, I-win-you-lose types of games to more complex situations in which all of the players could gain, or all could lose.[23] [24] It addresses the fact that outcomes in groups don't have to be zero-sum. In other words, in most corporate scenarios, one person's gain is not equivalent to another person's loss. Why? Because the constant assessments going on in our brains take into account that everyone else is also making assessments in and about the group benefits and their own self-interest—and this changes outcomes. It's a wonder we humans get any work done with this blizzard of assessments going on in our heads—but we do, because it helps us survive and thrive. This neurochemical process is vital to our survival. It works almost like our heartbeat—running in the background, imperceptibly keeping us alive without interfering with our ability to think about other matters at hand. It's pretty cool, and very powerful.

Beside the technical definitions of game theory, as a businessperson, I describe it as the bridge between self-interest and getting others to serve your self-interest in a group setting. Game theory studies this in practical scenarios, based on mathematical calculations and outcomes of how we come up with winning strategies in the game of life. Interestingly, Dr. John F. Nash is also the protagonist played by Russell Crowe in the popular movie *A Beautiful Mind*.[25]

Complex scenarios play out in our corporate offices and boardrooms every day as our human brains continuously assess the ever-important balance between self-interest and the interests of the group that we support in order to serve that self-interest. As a leader, you're doing the same thing as your people. You're part of the mix. And you know what? It's beautiful—complicated, but beautiful and logical. The problem is not our evolution; it's the fact that, as leaders, we've never been trained to understand, acknowledge, or respect evolutionary or biological truths about human behavior. In fact, all too often, we unknowingly fight against them, which makes our jobs much more difficult and sets us up for failure.

At its essence, game theory mathematically maps out how self-interest plays out in a group setting in a variety of common scenarios, especially around perceptions of fairness, cooperation, and power. While it is impossible to discuss the related literature in its entirety, it is worthwhile to review some relevant game theory models that can help us become better at interpreting the group dynamics we face as leaders of teams and projects.

## The Ultimatum Game

In the ultimatum game, two players are matched. Player A is given a sum of money, and Player B is given no money. Player A is asked to make an offer of money to Player B. If Player B accepts the offer, they both get their agreed upon amounts. If Player B rejects the offer, they both walk away with nothing. Player A has everything to lose, and Player B has everything to gain. One might think that Player B would accept any amount of money, but research shows this isn't the case. Research shows that offers below 25 percent are likely to be rejected—perhaps because the offer is seen as unfair. It appears Player B would rather sanction Player A for an unfair offer than walk away with less money than he or she feels they deserve. For this reason, Player A—who naturally wants to maximize what they keep—must consider Player B's idea of fairness in order to have the offer accepted. Rejections in this game can be seen as punishment for the proposer's violation of social norms. If Player A offers between 40 and 50 percent of the money, research shows the offer is almost always accepted. Perhaps that's why the 40 to 50 percent offer is also the most popular. It's lower risk. What's also interesting is that, as the game is repeated, players can build reputations. Player A can become seen as "fair," "unfair," or a "tough negotiator." Player B might be labeled as someone with a "history of rejection" or as a "pushover." These reputations can then influence and complicate offers in subsequent games.

## The Dictator Game

The dictator game is the ultimatum game with a twist. In the dictator game, only Player A decides how the money gets distributed. Player B can still accept or reject Player A's offer, but if Player B rejects the offer, Player A doesn't forfeit the money, only Player B loses out on the cash. In other words, Player B is completely at the mercy of Player A, the dictator. Research shows that in the dictator game, Player A's offer is significantly lower than it is in the ultimatum game. This is not surprising. There's much less of a need to make a "fair" offer. Player

A can simply maximize the cash take. Why give up anything when you can have everything, right? Well, it turns out to be a bit more complex than that. Research shows that Player A ends up offering Player B at least some money. Why? Player A certainly doesn't want to look like someone who disregards the universal understanding of fairness or oversteps social norms. Think about how you would feel if you intentionally mistreated someone who was unable to defend themselves. You would feel bad, right? This feeling is exactly the sort of evolutionary shortcut that compels us to behave fairly (most of us, at least). And why is that? Well, if you treat someone unfairly, it is likely to come back to haunt you. It can hurt your reputation in the group, which could alter your success in future rounds of the game. And if you treat many people unfairly, you could soon turn the entire group against you. This is not in your self-interest because, as we have already learned, being alone will not help you survive and thrive—not in the dictator game and not in the game of life. What's even more interesting is Player B often still rejects offers viewed as too low—even though he or she will end up with nothing. It's a sort of "You've gotta be kidding me" reaction. So far, so bad for Player B, right? But research also shows that when an offer is rejected, the next offer that Player A proposes is higher than in the previous round.[26] Why is this important? First, it shows that even when Player B stands to lose everything, they still want to make sure the dictator understands they made a mistake. Their message is, "You might have won all the money, but I hope you feel badly about it, buddy!" And we do feel badly, because our stingy offer was rejected. In the next round, we are likely to up our offer to ensure we're closer to acceptable norms as well as to avoid building a negative reputation, which others can and will use against us.

## The Sanction Game

Another adaptation of the ultimatum game, called the sanction game, adds to the mix. In this game, a Player C is tasked with sanctioning Player A if his or her offer is deemed too low. To make things more interesting, Player C also receives part of the money. If Player

C were only interested in his or her own financial distribution, there would be no reason to sanction unfair offers. However, not only does research show that Player C penalizes Player A for unfair behavior, but the penalty rises inversely in proportion to the perceived unfairness. In other words, the lower the offer, the higher the penalty. Another interesting research finding shows that when Player B learns to expect Player C to penalize low offers by Player A, they begin to collaborate. And since players never know when Player A's actions will impact them or someone they care about, they decide to put an end to Player A's unfair activity. If everyone knows something is unfair, they expect those who can do something about the unfairness to indeed do something about it.

## Game Theory in the Office

Now, let's take all of these games into the office. Certainly, there's plenty of weighing of what's fair and unfair in a professional setting. There is also the continuous assessment by everyone of everyone's reputations—colleagues, bosses, and subordinates. Who's a jerk? Who always gets the job done? Who plays well with others? You get the idea. Add a healthy dash of evolutionary self-interest into this mix and things start to get really interesting.

Understanding people's positions and reputations is important, whether you're in leadership or not. This knowledge heavily influences our decision-making process and behavior in a group setting. For example, if people see you as a "tough cookie," they are likely to approach you carefully to ensure they get what they want—or maybe they don't approach you at all. While this may have benefits in some circumstances, it can be a burden in others. Similarly, if you are trying to get a project funded and you know the person who sits in the right-hand corner of the conference room is always the roadblock, you will probably go to that person first and see what they're willing to give. At that point, you can accept what they offer, negotiate for a bit more, or stubbornly stand your ground and possibly lose everything. Or, if a colleague treats you unfairly, you might sanction them by quietly refusing to support their efforts. If that colleague offends enough people, they will probably struggle to build support for future professional projects and ideas. Conversely, if a subordinate says something insensitive in a meeting that you're running, you might try to help them read the room better, rather than snap at them. This behavior not only helps your subordinate, it also helps you establish a reputation as a benevolent leader. Whereas, if you had you snapped at the subordinate, you might have been seen as cruel, unfair, or arrogant. But if a peer acts out in a meeting, you will probably challenge them, because if you don't, folks might see you as weak. And if you challenge someone above your level in the company, you might even be perceived as brave. As a leader, these "games" are being played out around you every minute of every day—and you are part of them. Meanwhile, you're doing your own assessments and learning to process and manage all the other reputation inputs from your subordinates, colleagues, and bosses. Though you will never play the game perfectly, you must keep learning and continue improving—even as the corporate environment around you continues to change.

Where does this leave us? Human nature is not the enemy—our lack of knowledge of human nature is. Research has taught us:

1.  Humans incentivize group-friendly behavior because it helps the individual survive and thrive.

2.  Humans penalize antigroup behavior because it can put stress on productive group behavior, which in turn jeopardizes individual members' success.

3.  Humans feel good when they do good. We are wired to support the group in order to support ourselves. We reward "team players" even if they are driven by self-interest.

4.  Humans feel bad when their expectations of others are not met.

5.  Humans don't like inequality, which can come in two ways: having more than someone else or having less. Humans are extremely sensitive to the latter.[27]

6.  Humans do not allow themselves to be exploited (at least voluntarily). They will not sacrifice their own needs for those of the group if they can't see benefits for themselves or the people close to them (mainly family).

7.  The human brain is constantly assessing the risk-reward ratio when it comes to group participation. It is not a zero-sum game because all the individuals in the group are doing the same thing.

This is how we humans are wired. We are constantly assessing whether the benefits of the group support our self-interest.[28] [29] [30] [31] We continue to serve and nurture the group if we feel that it does, and we leave or pull away if we feel it does not. As a leader, nothing is more important than understanding this evolutionary concept. Leaders who recognize the individuality of all group participants nurture successful group behavior because they show how working as an aligned group helps these individuals achieve their own goals. I have been a part of many groups over the course of my career, and here is what I have seen firsthand: the highest performing groups—the groups that thrive for the longest period, and also are the most fun—are all groups where the talents and growth of the individuals in the group are highly appreciated. It didn't matter if I was a member or leader of the group, the respect for individuality created an environment in which everyone could survive and thrive. This, in turn, ensured that the group would survive and thrive.

**Altruism and Game Theory**

The term *human altruistic cooperation* is defined as intensive activities that result in fitness, relevant to the economic advantages of other humans. It's unique among all the species, and it's very powerful. In fact, it's vital for human cooperation. Here are just four behavioral qualities of this phenomenon:

1. **Kin selection** means individuals engage in self-cost intensive behavior that benefits the genetic fitness of their relatives (and therefore of their own).

2. **Reciprocal altruism** is useful in situations where repeated interactions are very likely—like at work.

3. **Strong reciprocity** is a combination of reciprocal altruistic reward behavior for norm-conform and reciprocal altruistic penalty behavior for norm-inadequate behavior. Strong reciprocators sustain even costs for reward and penalty in situations when no direct fitness-relevant advantages occur. This behavior stands in clear contradiction to reciprocal altruistic behavior, which occurs only when at least one long-term individual interest is likely to be satisfied. Strong reciprocators always reward cooperation and penalize noncooperative behavior.

4. **Altruism based on reputation** occurs when other members of the same society experience another member as a reliable and consistent partner. This kind of reputation can be achieved if an individual, over the course of many interactions, proves themselves to be considerate and responsible. This earns increasing trust.

Now enter game theory, which allows us to explore how these altruistic behavioral qualities come into play when humans interact with different stakes on the table, as they say. For those who want to know more about this topic, I encourage you to read "Strong Reciprocity, Human Cooperation, and the Enforcement of Social Norms," published in the journal *Human Nature* in 2002.

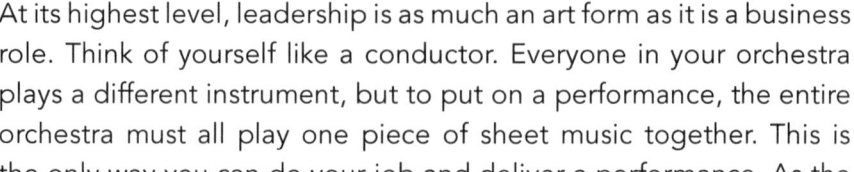

At its highest level, leadership is as much an art form as it is a business role. Think of yourself like a conductor. Everyone in your orchestra plays a different instrument, but to put on a performance, the entire orchestra must all play one piece of sheet music together. This is the only way you can do your job and deliver a performance. As the conductor, you know the most impressive music is produced when each individual instrument is played beautifully but every musician is following the sheet music and doing their part to the best of their ability. This is how harmony is achieved and standing ovations are inspired. You face a similar balancing act in business. You must support the individual in his or her endeavor to accomplish something unique while also serving the group in its effort to achieve something important together. So, when a strong leader is told that organizations can only thrive when everyone ignores their own unique interests and puts the organizations first, he or she ignores it. A good leader recognizes, celebrates, nurtures, develops, and champions differences in the talents, experiences, aspirations, and personalities of the team members. In celebrating individuality over sameness, the successful leader is able to align everyone around a common goal. There is complete buy-in because each individual has been seen and valued, and they understand they are being led to achieve a common goal that will benefit them all—both as a group and as individuals. *This* is what drives successful organizations to reach their goals—not sameness.

The good leader allows the members of their team to ask the question, "What's in for me?" The answer to this question allows the goals of the individual to coexist with the goals of the group. Call it two plus two makes five. The combination creates something greater than its sum. Groups and organizations become better when the individuals in these groups and organizations are encouraged to become better. And a good leader knows that people become better when they know why they are in the game. Your people need to know why it's worth it, *first* for them, *then* for the company—not the other way round. Good leaders know this is the formula for healthy, high-achieving teams and companies.

This formula also applies to you as an individual who leads other individuals. You have to know what you want to achieve and why the leadership journey you're on is worth it. But there's extra weight on you as a leader. Like the conductor, when the show begins, all eyes are on you. The musicians are looking for your direction to guide them through the musical piece, and the audience is looking at you throughout the performance. They're assessing the quality of your performance and your reputation as a conductor. It's a lot of pressure. The stakes and the stress are higher for you, so let's make sure you're ready to perform at the top of your game. It's what you're expecting from your people, and what your people are expecting from you.

# Chapter 1

# Fix Yourself First

## Mens Sana in Corpore Sano

*Mens sana in corpore sano. Orandum est ut sit mens sana in corpore sano.* Loosely translated from Latin, the first phrase means *a sound mind in a sound body*. The second phrase means that a man should pray for a healthy mind in a healthy body. Juvenal, a Roman poet who lived between 60 and 130 AD wrote this as part of a satire titled *Satire X*, later imitated by English author Samuel Johnson with his piece titled *The Vanity of Human Wishes*.[32] [33] Historical research reveals that he was not writing about sports, health, or fitness, nor was he proposing physical and mental perfection. Rather, he wanted people to understand that health is more important than the false benefits of greed and vanity. Today we say that "a healthy mind lives in a healthy body."

A growing body of research suggests that executive leaders, who deal with immense levels of responsibility and stress, often struggle to keep themselves mentally and physically fit. How leaders respond to this challenge has a clear correlation with their company's performance.[34] If you're a leader who is in tip-top shape, you'll be familiar with the lessons in this chapter. But if you're part of the majority who struggle to balance the pressures of work with time for self-care, this chapter is important for you to read carefully.

As a leader, staying fit and healthy shows your team that you have self-respect and self-discipline. You have an opportunity to demonstrate healthy behaviors and show your team that you respect yourself enough to take care of your mind and body. You can also inspire them by modeling how professional success can coexist with a balanced personal and family life. If you succeed in this type of role modeling, your coworkers and employees are likely to respect you, which means they are also likely to follow you and give their best to the team.

On the flip side, if you want your leadership to be sustainable and your impact on others to be lasting, it's not an option to eat the wrong food every day, skip workouts and sleep, or neglect your family. Justifying this lack of self-respect and self-discipline will not fly with your coworkers and team. It will make you a less effective leader. It's time to look in the mirror and ask yourself a few honest questions:

- How often do you come home late from a long day at work and tell yourself that you are too tired to work out?

- How often do you eat junk food after a long, stressful day?

- When you're traveling, how often do you order a big burger and beer sent to your room instead of going down to the hotel restaurant for a healthier meal that includes vegetables?

- How often do you drink at night just to calm down?

■   How often are you logging less than six hours of sleep at
    night?

If you answered even one or two of these questions with "once or
twice a workweek," you are in trouble—maybe not today, but certainly in the near future. Why? Because your health will gradually
deteriorate, and you will eventually become unhappy with yourself.
Your energy, focus, and self-esteem will suffer. Sooner or later, you
will look in the mirror and say, "This is not the me I used to be, and I
don't like it." Your doctor will tell you that you need to change your
lifestyle or will prescribe lifestyle-counteracting medications (think
statin or beta blockers). Your partner may tell you that he or she
misses the attractive, high-energy version of you. None of this is
good. When you neglect yourself and your personal life, you jeopardize your health, self-esteem, and relationships. At some point,
all of this will come back to bite you, diminishing your leadership
and decision-making capabilities. This is how burnout happens, and
that's going to hurt you and the team that relies on you. Ultimately,
your career will suffer.

Let's flip this and think about how great you would feel if you worked
out several days a week, ate healthy and balanced meals, logged at
least seven hours of sleep at night, and spent more time with your
family and friends. There is plenty of scientific evidence demonstrating that these actions will make you a better version of yourself. This
type of lifestyle also has consequences—and they are all positive.

That voice in your head says, "Yes, I get it, but I spend 50 percent
of my time traveling. I have a lot of responsibility and an enormous
workload with constant deadlines and pressures." Most likely, you
can't finish everything in a forty-hour workweek. I get it. This has been
the reality of my entire professional life too. But I'm not advising that
you become a world-class athlete or Olympian. I just want to share
with you a few simple rules that will help you feel and function better

in your career and life. I follow these rules and they have helped me tremendously. Let's start with exercise.

## Creating an Exercise Habit

I've been athlete my entire life. As a result, I've adhered to a no-matter-what, six-days-a-week workout regimen since I was in my late teens. But in 2014, I signed up with a group of folks to compete in the Little Debbie Ironman in Chattanooga, Tennessee. The event raised funds for many different causes, and the cause my team was participating for was the American Crohn's and Colitis Foundation. Yes, I was used to rigorous, daily workouts. But my usual training was not enough for this event. During my yearlong preparation for the Ironman, I logged 220 hours on the bike, 113 hours of running, and 85 hours in the water—and I haven't even mentioned the hours I spent commuting to these workouts. I did all of this in addition to my "normal" job, which required me to be on call 24/7 and travel internationally on a regular basis. I accomplished my goal and finished the Ironman, but the extra training was quite a challenge. I share this story because, like you, I know how hard it can be to keep everything in balance while trying to achieve your personal and professional goals as well as take care of yourself, your team, your family, and your friends.

I'm not asking anyone to train for an Ironman, like I did. That was a personal choice. I just want to share with you three simple rules to integrate regular exercise into your hectic workweek while preserving important quality time for family and friends. If you master these simple rules, not only will you see a positive impact on your health and well-being, you will also improve your leadership capabilities. No matter how busy you are, these tips can lead to positive, sustainable, and long-lasting behavioral changes that will improve the quality of your personal and professional life.

## Rule 1: Rhythm Before Volume

Life is all about rhythms. The best way to change a rhythm or start a new rhythm is to keep the barrier to entry as low as possible. Why? Because when an activity is simple, our ability to sustain that activity is very high. Pick a time to work out that you know you can keep. It might be first thing in the morning, at lunch, or after work. Commit to working out at that time for fifteen to thirty minutes three times a week, at most. Do not commit to anything more! In other words, don't work out longer or add workout days. Stick to this routine for at least six weeks. Why not do more out of the gate? There are many reasons, but let's start with the top two:

1.  You could injure yourself if you don't give your body the time it needs to acclimate to this new routine.

2.  You could start resenting the new routine because it's too much, too soon. If you suddenly add an hour of exercise to your workday five times a week, you could throw off your schedule and cause yourself (and possibly others) stress.

All too often, people who push too hard and too fast end up quitting after a few weeks or become what I call "weekend warriors." These people work out for a couple of hours every Saturday and Sunday, trying to make up for the exercise rhythm that they have never established. They hit the gym on both weekend days, push their heart rates too high on cardio, and try to lift the same amount of weight they were able to lift in their twenties. After they've almost killed themselves, they hit the sauna for forty-five minutes to recover. To accomplish weekend warrior status, they miss family gatherings and push themselves too hard—neither is good for their health, nor does it help them achieve work-life balance. Sooner, rather than later, this leads to negative feelings—stress, resentment, a sense of failure or dread. Being a weekend warrior is much too complicated and unlikely to lead to long-term success. It's much better to start with a sustainable workout routine that helps you feel successful quickly.

Watch that aerobic exercise program for beginners. Ride that bike that you bought two years ago but never used. Walk on the tread-mill at your company's gym. What are the likely outcomes of this approach? Here are the top two:

1.  Instead of feeling exhausted and frustrated, you'll feel in-vigorated. These positive, post workout emotions will en-courage you to repeat the behavior and stick to your new, sustainable routine.

2.  Instead of risking injury, your body will grow stronger each week. This will encourage positive feelings of success and empowerment.

After six to eight weeks of benefits and positive reinforcement, you may feel comfortable in your new routine. It's a habit that you now look forward to throughout the week. At this point, you might be ready for more. Then, and only then, does it make sense to increase the amount of time you work out or the frequency of those workouts. Do not, however, fall into the trap of increasing one training each week to ninety minutes while leaving the others at twenty minutes. Instead, increase the entire rhythm, maybe by five to ten extra min-utes. Let your body ask for more. Wait until you have the feeling that the routine is part of you—you love it and can't imagine giving it up. That's when you can think about increasing the length or intensity of your workout or incorporating a new exercise. Remember, rhythm before volume.

## Rule 2: Integration of Duties

We've all heard it, and we've all said it: "I don't have time to work out." This may seem true as you stare at the pile of work on your desk, but it is most definitely false. We always have time for work, don't we? Here's what I propose: integrate work and your workout into one activity. Let's say that on the Thursday of your third week of your new twenty-minute elliptical workout regime, you find out that you have an important presentation on Friday morning in front of key leaders in your company. It's a big deal. Do you skip the elliptical training to prepare? You don't have to choose, because you can do both with a bit of planning. Here's how I handle these situations. I prepare the slides in advance of my workout and then print them out on double-sided sheets, with two slides per page. I take the printouts with me to the gym, rest them in front of me on the elliptical, and start pedaling. While I'm pedaling, I go through my presentation in my head. My workout flies by, and when I finish, I feel great! Against all odds, I have prepared for my presentation without interrupting my exercise regimen. I know this is possible because I do it all the time.

## Rule 3: Monitor Your Progress

Write down what you do, at least for the first few months. This can be as easy as sending yourself an email or writing in a notebook. Simply document what exercise you did, when you did it, and for how long. Alternatively, put your smartwatch to use, if you have one. It will keep you honest! After a few weeks, you'll see with your own eyes that you stuck to your new exercise regime. You can see the rhythm and feel the benefits. You see the calories burned, the sleep improved, etc. Your commitment is paying off. It has become part of your weekly behavior. Yes, sometimes life will disturb the rhythm of your new behavior, but that won't throw you off course because you will be so committed that you'll find a way to fit in that workout the next day. You'll miss your routine and want to find a way to retain this rhythm of success, albeit with a slight adjustment. Once something is a true behavior, fitting it in becomes much easier and more manageable.

Those are my three simple rules about exercise. Adhere to them because they work. Not only will these tips improve your work-life balance, but they will also improve your stamina as a business leader and help you perform better no matter what your job throws at you.

## Feed Your Ambitions

Of course, this is a leadership book, not a diet book. But let's be honest, you don't need another diet book; you know perfectly well what is healthy to eat and what is not. The choice to eat bad food often resembles the justification for why people don't work out. It typically goes something like this: "Today was so hard and long. I didn't even have a chance to eat anything. I'm tired, hungry, and I still have work to do. I don't have time to prepare something healthy. I'm just going to order chicken wings, fries, and a Coke. It's easy and I've got to eat something fast, right?" Wrong! How does not having the opportunity to eat translate into justification for a decision to put toxic stuff inside your body? That mental jump is not the least bit logical. It's like saying it's okay to fill up the empty gas tank of your car with diesel fuel because that's the only type available. That doesn't make any sense!

Let's be clear: unhealthy decisions are rarely about a lack of time or options. They are about a lack of self-respect and self-discipline. Unhealthy decisions mean you are prioritizing the wrong things. If you find yourself regularly making unhealthy food decisions, you need to replace this damaging behavior with a healthy one. I don't mean to be harsh, but as a leader, you must regularly look in the mirror and take stock. We all have work to do on ourselves. We all have areas where we could do better. That's a given. That's being human. You must become self-aware and commit to ongoing self-improvement. How can you lead others if you can't lead yourself? Step away from the junk food and order a decent meal. You're worth it.

Luckily, there is an easy fix: the same three rules we used to start a healthy exercise regime apply for food as well.

## Rhythm Before Volume

Don't change everything in your diet. Instead, make a few simple healthy substitutions and stick to them a few days a week. Start small, aim for consistency, and begin experiencing the benefits of success. Even substituting water for soda will have a positive health impact in a short amount of time.

### Integration of Duties

If you have a long meeting that cuts into dinner, skip the pizza—order a healthy meal for your team instead. This takes minimal planning and can make a big difference over time. It will help you eat better and be a role model at the same time. If you're traveling, there are plenty of healthy options for eating out or in. Stop making excuses and start making healthy choices.

### Monitor Your Progress

Keep a food journal to hold yourself accountable. There are plenty of apps to help with this as well. Once your activity has become a reliable behavior after six or more weeks, you can start adding a few new healthy food substitutions to improve even more.

Make the right choices: exercise, eat right, and get a decent night's sleep. If you struggle to commit to simple new routines of self-care, perhaps it's time to consider professional help. Being a leader takes incredible courage. Ask yourself this: Is it braver to ignore what's holding you back in life than it is to identify and address these issues head-on? I think not. As Kenneth Blanchard, renowned management consultant and author of *The One Minute Manager*, famously said, "Asking for others' guidance helps you see what you may not be able to see. It's always important to check your ego and ask for help."

## Anchor Yourself

Once you have taken care of your body, it's time to think about your sanity. I'm only half joking. When juggling the demands of your leadership role, you must, as they say, mind your mind. In today's fast-paced world, that's not easy; the juggling act just keeps getting crazier.

Yes, we're wired to multitask in groups, and we do it every day in our jobs. But as hunters and gatherers in the early days of our evolution, we humans worked primarily in small groups with a focus on one or two straightforward goals. Natural borders like mountains and rivers kept our small groups separated most of the time, which is one reason why things stayed pretty much the same for hundreds of thousands of years. Then, during the Neolithic Revolution, we humans started to specialize and settle down together in larger groups. Still, change happened slowly. For thousands of years, the harsh realities of survival kept us focused on achieving a small number of goals, like putting food on the table and keeping roofs over our heads, with a relatively small group of people.

The modern world, however, is like a giant neural network, keeping us connected and communicating 24/7, 365 days a year. Messages travel from office to office, building to building, state to state, and country to country at the speed of light. There is nothing obstructing the constant stream of inputs that can be sent and received through our mobile phones, social media, meeting technology, and so forth. Additionally, these rapid technological developments have allowed us to create and participate regularly in much larger groups—national clubs, multinational corporations, and multicountry organizations to name just a few. And these larger groups can focus on numerous complex goals: strategic initiatives, financial benchmarks, performance targets, cultural working groups, social programs—the list goes on and on. Our hunter-gather brains aren't wired for all this—and yet we're forced to deal with it every day.

We've all experienced it: You leave your desk for a quick lunch and come back to almost twenty emails. Among them is an "urgent request" from someone in your organization you've only met once. No matter, it's important, so you drop everything—even though you're supposed to be prepping for an important Zoom meeting with another team on the other side of the world. At the same time, you're checking your phone every two minutes, hoping to get a text that says the crucial information you need for that meeting is finally in your inbox. Meanwhile, an alert comes through on Slack that someone has updated the calendar invite and moved the meeting up twenty minutes to accommodate someone's schedule on the other team. This means you won't be prepared to deliver the information needed to finally close the project that you so badly want to get off your desk. Needless to say, you are stressed out because none of this is in your control. You just have to react and deal with it all, and quickly.

This is just how business is done in the modern world. We are no longer in charge of our daily activities to the extent we once were. Increasingly, it seems reversed: our daily activities are in charge of us. Life feels a bit out of control. There's a sense of losing ourselves in the madness of it all. And don't think for one second that this goes away as you move up the corporate ladder. The higher you rise in an organization and the more people you lead, the more you risk losing control of your life. Leading more people and more groups means dealing with more complexity, and there's a higher probability of a wild card interrupting your schedule. Meanwhile, as a rising leader, you're taking on more responsibility and ceding more control to HQ's way of doing things. It's a lot to manage, both professionally and personally.

How do you cope? Anchor yourself.

Outside of work, always do something that really matters to you. Something that fulfills your inner desire for a higher purpose. Unlike other species on this planet, we humans have the ability to be part of different social systems at the same time. We can work during the day and join a local soccer team, chess club, or painting class at night or on the weekends—whatever floats our boat. Moreover, we can play different roles and have different ranks within these separate social systems. In other words, organizations outside of work may offer us less complexity, more control, and higher status. Anchoring yourself with such activities is a proactive way to balance the chaotic days you experience as a leader at work.

It also feels good to learn something new and become good at something. That's human nature. Maybe you're an aspiring or seasoned musician, athlete, gardener, community organizer, fisherman, or artist. You should never shelve your talents and dreams just because your workday is hectic. To the contrary, they should be fostered. Not only do they provide a sense of accomplishment, they can also ground you as you navigate the choppy waters of corporate leadership. All humans crave self-efficacy and admiration. As a product-manager associate, you might prepare other people's slides all day, but when you head to the martial arts club at night, people admire your discipline and talent. As a business unit director haunted by a general manager who is only interested in his P&L, you know when you leave work, you'll be a sought-after assistant professor of art history at the local community college. As an insurance sales rep who archives key performance indicators in the company's CRM to satisfy HQ's latest bullshit initiative, you can shake it all off at the stables where you're on your way to becoming an Olympic contender in dressage. And, by the way, these are all real-world examples.

If you want to stay sane as a corporate leader, you must have at least one activity outside of work that you can be proud of—something where others look up to you for your expertise, advice, and leadership. That sense of control and accomplishment will make you happier and more confident. It will also strengthen your coping skills and fortify you for the tough workdays ahead. It will give you an anchor that no one can take away.

## It Is Not about You

Have you ever had a manager who tries to one-up you on everything? You tell them you just got a dog, and they turn around and say they already have two. You talk about an interesting article; they email you one they say is more interesting. You bring up an important point in a meeting; they counter with an observation they say is even more important.

You know the type.

They post quasihumble messages on LinkedIn to let everyone know about their latest and greatest "academic" adventures and achievements, like the shortcut Ivy League university program they just completed—all funded with their management-level salary, which they keep reminding you is much higher than yours. In meetings, they are the loudest and speak the most. If you challenge them, they take it personally, because they always have to be right. Even when they show interest in others' opinions, everyone knows it's fake and driven by some underlying scheme to make themselves look better. When someone is in charge of hundreds of employees, they should be practicing humility and supporting their team members. The LinkedIn posts should be about the people they lead, not about themselves.

If you've ever been managed by someone like this—and most of us have at least once in our careers—you know firsthand how frustrating this type of ugly, immature behavior can be. It destroys individual and team morale. As a leader, if you ever find yourself slipping into selfish, narcissistic patterns, stop and remember how that former manager made you feel back in the day. Then, remind yourself of this mantra every day: it's not about you. The most important ground rule for an effective leader is this: It's not about your interests, opportunities, or achievements. It's not about how great or clever *you* are. It should always be about your people and what they can and are achieving. It should always be about them. When you go into leadership meetings, let your team present. When you are asked to present on behalf of your team, start by reminding everyone that the presentation is your people's work. When things go right, they did it. When things go wrong, you take the blame for them. As Simon Sinek famously said, "Leaders eat last!"[35] Never forget that it's not about you.

# Practice Authentic Confidence and Self-Awareness

There's a popular notion in the business world that leaders need to be tough.

"Don't go all soft on me, Larry. Have a backbone!"

"Toughen up, Lucy. This is what managers do."

"Take my advice: You always have to be a little mean to your sales reps. They'll respect you more." (Yes, someone actually said this to me at a corporate dinner.)

You've probably heard something similar at least once in your career. Being perceived as "strong," "in charge," or "hard" can be a sort of badge of honor in certain corporate cultures. When that's the case, power displays can be seen all around the office. Bosses practically break your hand when they shake it. Directors proudly display their boxing gloves behind their desks. General managers plop their feet up on the desk and leave the office door open so everyone can see their power posturing. This is not confidence; it's hubris—a form of exaggerated and false confidence. Psychologists tell us such behaviors are overcompensation for low self-esteem. Authentic confidence emanates from self-awareness and a commitment to ongoing personal growth. We're all human. We all have our issues. But when someone is promoted into a leadership position, they become responsible for business performance, people's livelihoods, and the professional development of others. True leaders commit to the continuous personal work required to become a better person for themselves and others. You can't fake authentic confidence or self-awareness. You must do the hard work. It's not optional if you want to be a successful leader.

How do hubris and a lack of self-awareness impact a team and its performance? Before sharing my answer, I ask you to keep something in mind: typically, people aren't promoted because of their self-awareness or their understanding of human behavior; they are promoted because someone thinks they have excelled in a particular role, accomplished an important goal, or demonstrated a specific and useful skill. Sometimes people reach leadership positions because the person hiring them knows that this new "leader" won't challenge them. As a result, all too often, people with low self-esteem, little self-awareness, overconfidence, or all of the above are promoted into leadership positions they're not fit to handle. When this new "leader" arrives for his or her first day on the job, everyone pays close attention and forms a first impression that sticks. When this new boss struts overconfidently into the office, starts bragging about their tough management style and stellar business record, and then tells everyone to step it up because it's time to right the ship, well, everyone knows exactly what's coming next—trouble! Immediately, the whole team starts to adapt. People think twice about calling out obvious strategic failures the department or company is about to make. Why? Because they know the new boss won't want to hear it and heads will roll. Team members begin strategizing in small groups about how to phrase things so as not to irritate the new boss. Important information, observations, and ideas go unshared. There's no professional development. Instead, everyone is walking on eggshells. It's unlikely a team will thrive under this type of pressure. It's only a matter of time before people start leaving and performance drops off. Don't be that "leader." Confront your demons, work on your weaknesses, and hone your strengths. The journey toward authentic confidence and self-awareness is never-ending, but it's a journey every successful leader must take.

# Always Be Kinder Than Necessary

What's the antidote to hubris and bravado in the workplace? It might seem obvious, but it's actually often overlooked, perhaps because it's so simple: be kinder than necessary. Ignore anyone who tells you to be tough. That's their insecurities speaking. Great teams are led by true leaders who are rational, kind, helpful, and humble. Sir James Matthew Barrie, also known as J.M. Barrie, was a Scottish novelist and playwright best remembered for creating Peter Pan. He said it best: "Be kinder than necessary because everyone you meet is fighting some kind of battle." There is so much truth in those fourteen words. As leaders, we can never know all the struggles our people are facing. Why pile on additional burdens with bad behavior that comes from our own struggles? There is always an opportunity in leadership to become a better person, to continually evolve toward our best selves. This means showing empathy and kindness. That's not being too soft; it's being smart, because when people feel genuinely appreciated, understood, and respected, they perform better.

One of the greatest compliments I received in my career was from a general manager whom I still highly respect. Many years ago, he told a room full of people that I get right the one thing every manager needs to get right: to be kind and nice. I was blown away by this. I still know exactly where this moment happened and exactly who was in the room. It was one of my proudest leadership moments. But believe me, I don't always get it right. There was another memorable moment when one of my direct reports told me, "You are a tough man." At the time, I was in a very difficult leadership role. I could have just told myself that the end justifies the means and moved on. But that comment hurt. As clearly as I remember the compliment from my general manager about being kind and nice, I remember exactly when and where the "tough man" comment happened. I recall distinctly that this manager did not say, "Nicolas, you can be tough sometimes" or "You can come across as tough at times." He said, "You are a tough man." As a leader, I knew this was bad. I had work to do.

So how can we be kind and nice and still get our points across? Is this even possible? Of course, it is. Dr. Henry Cloud, author of *Boundaries for Leaders*, said it this way: "Be hard on the issue but soft on the person."[36] By this, he meant have high standards but have a warm approach to feedback, especially when things go wrong. There are many advantages to this approach. It allows you to maintain strong relationships with your people while encouraging positive change. It increases trust, which is the main currency of leadership. It helps you build a reputation as a fair and approachable leader, which means people will tell you the truth, even when it's not what you want to hear. They will also share their opinions and ideas. You might not always agree with them, but at least you've learned from their perspective—even when you respectfully agree to disagree at the end of the conversation. All of this will help you become a better leader and make better decisions. Over time, this will translate into better performance and stronger outcomes. Kindness and empathy are the hallmarks of a great leader.

# Chapter 2

# Build *Your* Team

Earlier in the book, we talked about taking care of yourself and becoming more self-aware—both foundational for strong leadership. Recognizing that you are an individual leading a team of individuals—all with a healthy sense of self-interest—is an important step in embracing evolutionary truths. Wise leaders don't try to deny their own self-interest or those of their team members. That approach never works. Learning how to manage the complex dance of self-interest and group dynamics in a fast-moving environment requires continuous learning. If you're doing the hard work to grow as a leader, then you've probably been tasked with team building. So, in this chapter, we're going to help you start building *your* team, not just *any* team—*yours*!

# Bring at Least One Lieutenant

As you step into your first leadership role or advance to a higher one, you are likely taking over someone else's team. Either the former leader is moving to a new department, is leaving the company, or was fired. Once in a great while, you get to build a new team from scratch, but most of the time you are inheriting a team—and this comes with unique challenges and opportunities.

Keep this important fact front and center, especially in the first year: the team you are about to lead is the *other* person's team—not yours. This will change over time if you are a strong leader. In the beginning, though, you're going to have to build trust, fortify relationships, and assess the strengths, weaknesses, and potential development needs of each member of your inherited team. All of this is necessary to shape this group of people into the team you need to do your job well. It's not an easy task, but it's crucial for your success and theirs.

Therefore, my number one rule for leaders inheriting a team is this: find someone you can trust completely—100 percent! You can bring them in from a past project or company or develop this person from within your new team. Either way, find a person who will stick with you no matter what—someone who has your back and will be honest with you. They should share your core values and have a positive attitude. While there are advantages to bringing in someone you already know, like experience working together, this is not a necessity. If you decide to choose someone from within the new team, don't just look at their resume. You need to ensure this person has the necessary skills, yes, but I always prefer a stellar attitude over the right CV. One of my earliest managers taught me a very important leadership lesson. There is only one thing that differentiates a high-performing employee from a low-performing employee: attitude. If a team member is open to learning and growth, they're going to be open to learning and growing with you as their new leader. If they don't have this attitude, that's going to be a roadblock. Choose someone with a stellar attitude, and then treat this new relationship with the care and respect it deserves. Whomever you choose, this new "lieutenant" will become part of your lifeline until this team you have inherited becomes truly yours, which takes time and nurturing.

## Listen to Your Gut

Even if every member of the team you inherit is highly skilled and experienced, these are not the main currencies humans trade in when it comes to relationships. Sometimes you just click with a person and sometimes you don't. First impressions are powerful, and your gut usually gives you a strong read as to whether you're going to like a person. The reasons for these gut reactions are complex and the science around them multifactorial. However, you don't need to study all the science behind gut reactions to know they exist and are mostly accurate. Why? Because you experience the gut's decision-making power every time you meet a new person. Behaviors, olfactory components, looks, past experiences, and reputation are just a few inputs that shape these initial gut reactions. Your gut's advice should play a big role in your hiring and firing decisions. Let me explain.

Throughout my career, I've had the opportunity to be involved in or make the final call on hundreds of hiring decisions. Most of the time, I made the right call and directly hired or helped to hire the right person for the job. I have always judged the success of such hires by these outcomes: the hire did good work, went on to have a successful career within the company (and beyond), and expressed that they were generally happy with the opportunities and professional development they experienced as an employee. In other words, it was a win for me, the company, and for them.

One achievement I'm especially proud of is that in every department and leadership role in my career—across all the years, positions, companies, industries, and countries—at least three-quarters of the people who reported to me moved on to bigger responsibilities and leadership roles during my tenure or afterward. Even more satisfying is that fact that some of the folks who joined my teams came with baggage from former management stating things like they were "not good enough" or had "low potential." I am happy to say that I saw them differently, gave them the opportunities and the environment they needed to develop themselves, and proudly watched them move on to bigger responsibilities in highly respected corporations. This gives me a strong sense of gratification. I like helping people achieve their full professional potential.

But no one is perfect, and I am by far no exception. Despite my strong track record, I did not get it right in a few cases. I made the wrong decision. I did not hire the right person for the job. These mistakes still haunt me. Every detail of those missteps is etched into my brain: the person's name, even the time and location where I made the decision to hire them, even though my gut sensed they were not the right fit. It's painful to get a hiring decision wrong. It weakens your position as a leader. It challenges the cohesiveness and performance of your team. It's not good for the employee either. After a while, once the writing is on the wall, you must move this person within or outside the company. The whole experience stings for everyone involved.

As a leader, you ask yourself, "Why did this happen? Where did I go wrong?" Since hindsight is always twenty-twenty, I can tell you *exactly* why specific hires did not work out. In every single case, I ignored what my gut was telling me. I overrode my instinct because I was impressed by the person's skills, experience, capabilities, interview performance, academic record, or something else. As a result, I forgot my cardinal rule: listen to your gut, Nicolas! I should never have brought any of them on, and my gut knew this even as I was making the hiring decision.

Let me be clear on two things: First, I'm not placing blame for my decisions on the employees that I hired. My point is not to say that these people were not capable of great things. They certainly were, and some of them moved on to very big responsibilities at other companies. Second, I'm not saying, "Just let your gut decide" or "Make unfiltered hiring decisions." What I am saying is that in a particular hiring moment for a particular organization and with my team's unique strengths and weaknesses at that time, my gut raised doubts. It told me that this person was not a fit for this particular circumstance. But instead of listening to this inner voice, I covered my ears and talked myself into each of these hires based on all the inputs swirling around me: their impressive skills, their deep experience, their glowing recommendations, etc. All of this took precedence in my decision to hire, even though my gut kept shouting, "Nicolas, don't do it!"

Over time, I became better at trusting my gut. Now, I share this piece of hard-earned wisdom with every leader I meet because you are allowed to listen to your gut. In fact, you have to once you have your "ideal" candidate on paper. This is exactly the moment when you need to stop and listen hard to what your gut is telling you. Let it be the final decision-maker. Our evolution has wired us to assess other humans, and we're pretty good at it. This, coupled with our professional experience, should be a trustworthy guide. In the end, the chemistry must be there, and that's what our gut is really good at recognizing. My advice couldn't be simpler: if your gut says no, listen!

The same is true when your gut tells you someone on the team you have inherited is not a good fit going forward. This is even tougher, because presumably, this person has been on the team for a while—and possibly has been with the company before you ever came along. But just because the last leader of the team felt this person was a good fit doesn't mean you have to feel the same way. It is highly unlikely you tick exactly the same way your predecessor did, so there could be a multitude of reasons why a person you inherited won't work out well on a team you're running. It's not an easy decision, but when you inherit a team, the job is to make it *yours*. That's why you must assess and make tough decisions about which team members will move forward with you. It's an important decision, so take your time, and remember to trust your gut.

After about six months of learning and analyzing the team you have been charged with leading, you'll likely begin to feel more confident and can assess if some positions need to change. Here are some of the reasons why you might want to move someone off your team:

1. You just don't connect with them. Maybe you have very different ways of looking at the business or life in general.

2. They think you took the job they deserved, and now they are resentful of the fact that they must report to you.

3. You discover your predecessor kept an underperforming member on the team because they were moving soon, and they didn't want to deal with the hassle of a complicated exit scenario.

4. You like someone but their talents don't fit your team's needs, and they are not performing well. As a result, you're spending too much time helping them. Is this even possible? Too much help? Yes, this is a problem because it breaks an important management-performance ground rule: spend most of your time with your highest performing people. If you spend too much time with low-performing team members—even if your intentions are honorable—it takes time and attention away from your highest performers. These high performers might feel slighted, which has the potential to decrease their performance or even cause them to leave your team. You don't want that to happen.

5.  Their behavior is destructive. Maybe they're screamers, fighters, unethical, rude, etc. You start to wonder, *Who is protecting this person?* However, most of the time, they are still in their position because someone was simply too cowardly to deal with them. Do not make the same mistake and hope the situation will improve. It won't. You might give one warning, but then they're gone. Call the HR team for instructions and then escort them out.

All these scenarios are different, but one thing should remain the same: if your gut tells you not to hire or keep a team member, listen carefully. You have been chosen to lead this team or department because people believe in your ability to deliver on their expectations. Don't let them, your team, and yourself down. To deliver on the promise others see in you, you need a high-performing team that you can trust and that trusts you. Do your homework, gather all the facts, and in that final decision-making moment, trust your gut!

## Trust You Must!

You've probably heard the saying, "Trust must be earned." Guess what? It's wrong. Scientific experiments around the world have shown that humans are naturally inclined to trust others, but they don't always.[37] Trust is given, at least a certain initial level, and then either strengthened or lost. This is how evolution made us. First, biologically, it has been proven that it is better to trust than not to trust. Over hundreds of thousands of years of evolution, humans have learned to read people, situations, and circumstances quickly. It is highly complicated, time-consuming, and inefficient to do extensive research before engaging in a business relationship. As an evolutionary shortcut, we have become highly skilled at reading body language for trust signals. For instance, when someone greets us with a slightly elevated hand showing their open palm, it tells us they have nothing in their hand and thus do not intend to harm us. We also look people in the eyes, check their posture, and assess their facial expressions, among other things. We only get suspicious if something is not "normal," as measured against a lifetime of daily experiences reading people.

Our default is to trust others and collaborate with them because it is in our best interest as individuals. Remember, evolution has taught us that together, we are stronger and more successful as a species. This doesn't mean we don't make mistakes when assessing other humans. But this is the exception, not the rule. When was the last time you asked the taxi driver for their driver's license before entering the car? Do you ask your dentist for his dentistry school certificates before you open your mouth? When you hired your last employee, did you call the university to see if the candidate really finished their courses with honors as stated on their resume? Probably not. But if someone behaves repeatedly in an unethical or destructive fashion, then trust is broken.

Trust is not earned; distrust is.

Successful leaders trust their people enough to give them the opportunity to make mistakes. Stumbling, learning together as a team, and improving after missteps are powerful trust-building experiences. I have always told my people that it's okay to make mistakes. I don't want them to be afraid to try new things or take risks. As a leader, it's my job to create a safe environment in which people can try things, stumble, learn from their mistakes, and grow. This is how great teams are built.

Trusting your employees and giving them the necessary freedom to try new things and make mistakes is a hallmark of successful leadership. Those who master this skill can lift their teams to ever-higher performance. Why? Because growth requires innovation, and innovation implicitly involves risk. Inevitably, in this creative cycle, there must be room for failure. Teams led by leaders who understand this and create a safe environment for inevitable failures allow innovation to thrive. In today's competitive marketplace, creating this type of an environment isn't just a luxury; it's a necessity. When a mistake happens, a good leader knows how to turn it into a learning moment. The team gets stronger and smarter because there is a process in place to assess mistakes, learn from them, and be better prepared for the next innovation.

Sometimes leaders struggle with the topic of trust and letting their people make mistakes. That stems from being part of too many corporate cultures that are highly risk and mistake averse. Most companies are ruled by all kinds of monitoring tools, dashboards, metrics, and key performance indicators. In fact, there are so many of these tools that people in big companies build entire careers around monitoring dashboards that force employees into transactional relationships with their leaders. "Give me a green dashboard and you get your incentive!" What ridiculous BS. I'm not saying to nix all dashboards or downplay the necessary role of key performance indicators. Data matter. I'm talking about managers who think these tools are the only gauge of success. Remember the Indemnify fiasco? That's an example of the limitations of dashboards because humans enter the data. Typically, "leaders" who are heavily dependent on dashboards do not trust their people and don't trust themselves to deal with mistakes. They only trust dashboards. Truth is, when these highly coveted management tools become leadership tools, they constantly fail.

During a management assessment long ago, I was accused by a "leadership consultant" of being too trusting of my people. Another assessment by one of the big shots of major consulting companies advised that my outcomes were so phenomenal, I must have pressured or incentivized my managers to achieve these high results. They reported this to my management team. Really? You cannot be serious!

As leaders, first and foremost, we must trust and empower our people. We must create a safe environment for them to innovate, fail, learn, and thrive. Key performance indicators and dashboards have their place. They can help us see certain problems, trends, and opportunities. But they don't provide the whole picture. They are management tools that should never be used as leadership tools. As leaders, trust is our most important tool. Never feel bad about trusting your people! Trust should lead, and leaders should trust.

## Do Not Invest in Your Competition

Albert Einstein once famously said, *"A person who never made a mistake never tried anything new."* As we've already discussed, your team must have the opportunity to take risks, make mistakes, and learn from them. It's your responsibility as a leader to build a safe environment in which employees don't fear repercussions every time there's a misstep. People can't innovate if they live in fear. *"All men make mistakes,"* Winston Churchill famously said, *"but only wise men learn from their mistakes." And that's the key, if everyone is learning, growing, and improving after their mistakes, you know you're doing something right.*

Of course, big miscalculations can have ripple effects. They can damage your team's reputation, your reputation, and even your company's reputation. You're undoubtedly going to take heat for larger missteps. Deep down, you might even want to fire the person who put you and your team in this situation. Don't do it. That's a bigger mistake. Let me clarify: think twice—or even better, three times—before firing somebody who made a mistake and learned from it. Only consider firing this person if he or she did not admit to the mistake, tried to blame others for it, or clearly learned nothing from the situation. Only then should you consider letting this person go. If someone repeats the same mistakes over and over, then you should consider whether they are right for the role. Otherwise, the culprit should stay. Why? Layoffs are costly—in terms of time, money, and knowledge lost. You need to invest in your people over the long term. Coached correctly, it's unlikely the culprit will make the same mistake twice. That's a big plus. And if you lay them off, you don't know which of your fierce competitors they'll join. Now *that* company has all of this former employee's hard-earned wisdom, and you're starting over with a new person. Additionally, no one on your team will remember anything from the big mistake now that this person is gone. Business will go on as usual and maybe a few changes will take place. But a year or two down the road, with potentially you yourself having moved on to another responsibility, your organization will probably make the same mistake again because nobody is there to remind everyone about the high cost that was paid the first time the mistake was made. As Winston Churchill famously said, when he was working to form the United Nations after World War II, "Never let a good crisis go to waste."

So, if you're thinking of firing someone for a mistake, even an expensive one, think again. You're setting yourself and your team up for a triple whammy: First, you already paid for the mistake. Second, you invested in your competition, which learned from your company's mistake because they hired the culprit. Third, your company will probably make the same mistake again. Congratulations, you've magnified the problem threefold. That's why, if at all possible, keep people who tried and failed! They learned something invaluable for the company!

## Appoint a Court Jester

Throughout history, court jesters have been known not only for their sharp tongues and quick wit but for their ability to use that wit to subtly call out bad behavior by the rich and powerful. They were granted comic dispensation because their criticisms were disguised as jokes, thus allowing the victims of their critiques to save face. The rich and powerful who employed court jesters also valued the hon-est, no-holds-barred feedback they received from them. Certainly, back when the royals were still shouting, "Off with their heads!" no one would dare tell the truth. Thus, court jesters became the best way for the rich and powerful to receive honest assessments about their decisions, character, actions, and reputation among the people.

As a leader, you're not running around shouting, "Off with their heads!" At least, let's hope not! However, you do hold significantly more power than those who report to you. In some ways, their fate is in your hands, and this makes people hesitant. They are unlikely to be completely honest with you when they think you've screwed up. That's human nature when the balance of power is unequal. But if you're surrounded by people who censor their responses, which is often the case in corporate environments, you're at risk of being out of touch with reality, which is never good.

That's why you need a court jester—someone who can speak the truth, uncensored, and keep you in check. In looking for your court jester, you must seek someone whom you trust implicitly, and they must feel the same way about you. This person must be very ma-ture and skilled in his or her own right, both from a leadership and a communication perspective. More importantly, this person must know how to stand firm even when your most narcissistic traits are on display. The court jester's job is to force you to look at yourself in the mirror every day, even when it's unpleasant—actually, *especially* when it's unpleasant. We all know that honest feedback decreases inversely to increases in responsibility, department size, and power. That's why a court jester becomes even more important as you rise in a company and get used to more and more positive feedback. When you walk on a stage to present in front of hundreds of people, there is often applause or a standing ovation. When you roll out the newest strategy backed up by all the numbers and analysis, every-one congratulates you and pats you on the back. You're on fire and walking on cloud nine. Then you get back to your office and your court jester walks in. "Don't kid yourself, that was BS!" They proceed to outline everything you did wrong and suggest ways you might improve. How does that taste? Well, not very good. Believe me, I've been there. But because there is trust between you and your court jester, and great respect, you listen, you assess, and you learn. It's in these conversations—not in the applause or the congratulatory messages—that you'll find opportunities to improve and grow as a leader.

Just a reminder: even as your court jester points out all your flaws and all the traps you fell into *again*, you must listen carefully *and* thank them for their constructive feedback. It's not always easy, but it's important. Sometimes, the truth will strain your relationship. That is why it is so important to choose the right person for the court jester job and be crystal clear with each other from the start about how this relationship is supposed to work. When the going gets tough, the strength of the relationship must pull you both through—the respect and mutual trust must be preserved. If this can be achieved, you are on to something invaluable that will shape you into a much stronger and wiser leader—your opportunities for growth become boundless.

I speak from personal experience. While it was not possible to establish this kind of relationship in every role I've had throughout my career, it was amazing when it did happen. You cannot imagine the lessons I learned through these relationships. I may have learned more from my court jesters than from my bosses. My court jesters kept me from running in the wrong direction and allowed me to harvest opportunities I was not able to see myself. They kept me from my self-fulfilling prophecies and opened doors for me to connect with important people I would have never known otherwise. My court jesters helped me grow and become a better leader. Though these relationships can sometimes be unpleasant and challenging, I encourage you to be brave and find a court jester for every team you lead. They will make you better!

One last note to make sure there's no confusion: a court jester and a lieutenant are not the same. A lieutenant is likely to share a lot of intangibles with you. There might be a natural chemistry, common interests, or a similar view of life. They might even be a friend. The court jester, on the other hand, should be your opposite, with different opinions on how to run the business. It's probably best not to bring a friend on as your court jester. Look for someone who respects you, is not threatened by you, and is willing to be brutally honest.

Just like in ages past when wise kings and queens had court jesters to keep them in check, so should today's wise leaders seek out a court jester. As entrepreneur, bestselling author, and speaker Seth Godin once said, "As our society gets more complex and our people get more complacent, the role of the jester is more vital than ever before. Please stop sitting around. We need you to make a ruckus."

## Hire for Your Blind Spot

When we make hiring decisions, we're looking for a certain profile—specific skills, knowledge, capabilities, and experiences. We let human resources filter the applications and give us a short list. We then let others narrow this list further through the interview process. Now it's our turn, and we're ready to sit down with the best candidates for that all-important one-on-one interview. What are we looking for? Fit—that combination of hard and soft skills that makes a person ready to hit the ground running, grow, and be successful on our team.

We're also assessing how this person will fit *in* with our team. Will their personality and behaviors mesh with others? In the early days of my career, this was a big focus for me. If I had a team of quick implementors, I hired people who could implement quickly. I was quick. The team was quick. The new hire had to be quick too. If I had a team of successful, scientifically focused sales reps, I looked for folks who would blend in and add grease to this already well-oiled machine. I was scientifically wired. My team was scientifically wired. Logically, we needed someone who was scientifically wired. Over time, however, experience taught me this was *not* the best way to hire. I completely changed my approach. I went from telling myself, "I need to hire someone who fits my team today" to "I need to hire someone who fits my team tomorrow, and this person needs to be able to help shape that tomorrow." I stopped trying to hire mirror images of myself and my team and started hiring for our blind spot.

Everyone and every team has a blind spot. I know mine, and hopefully you know yours. Today, I hire for my blind spot. If you and your team are quick decision-makers, hire someone who encourages you to think more fully and longer about your decisions, if needed, while not necessarily slowing you down. I bring on people with different perspectives and skills. This can come with its challenges, especially early on, but the payoff can be huge.

The bottom line is this: if you and your team are runners, do not hire a runner; instead, hire a climber who can show you and your team where to place the hooks in the wall. Initially, this might slow your team's pace, but you'll be ready to tackle mountains, not just straightaways, in the future. Don't hire a copy of yourself or your team. Hire for the future and where you want to go. Hire for your blind spot. It will reduce bias, increase emotional and intellectual bandwidth, and make you and your team better.

## Do Not Huddle Too Much

Have you ever been part of a great team that continuously outperformed all the other teams at your company? This team regularly exceeded targets, surpassed expectations, achieved the best possible outcomes, and redefined what is possible. If you have been part of a team like this, as I have been, you know it's an amazing experience.

There are compliments, promotions, high fives, bonuses, and elevated professional status. Everyone tells you how much they admire you and your team. They want to know how you've continued to achieve so much for so long. Be honest, who doesn't love all of *that*? People start to think that if you and your team can't do it, well, no one can! It's a great feeling.

You have all worked very hard to earn these accolades, and your accomplishments are certainly worthy of celebration. However, there are risks when this happens. You start thinking about success as a destination—and you guys have *definitely* arrived. Your team members start becoming a little complacent and stop challenging themselves. You all start believing your own victory story.

"Of course we'll close that deal. We *always* close those deals. We're amazing!"

"Of course we'll exceed our targets; we *always* exceed our targets. We rock!"

Yes, it's important to enjoy your success, but it's poison to start expecting it.

When your team starts to rest on your laurels, you're in trouble. That mindset will undermine all future success. It's like a slow-release poison, because when you think you are great, you stop trying to get better. That's the death knell for a high-performance team.

Luckily, there are some warning signs when your team becomes complacent. Everyone is getting cozy with one another. They always have one another's backs. Compliments are flying. And everyone starts to agree . . . all the time.

I call this huddling too much—and it's a symptom of a bigger problem.

On the surface, it seems great. Everyone is getting along. The atmosphere is upbeat and positive. But then one day, you are all together at a team meeting to work through a big challenge, and someone says, "We've tried everything," and the whole room nods in agreement. Or, when the first suggestion presented to solve a complex business case gets unanimously approved as is. Remember this moment, because it is *exactly* the one when your team turned south. If you don't turn this around, it's also the beginning of the end of your long winning streak.

Sound dramatic? It's not, because here's the secret sauce of success: friction—and your team has lost it. Questioning ideas and arguing through different scenarios and solutions is part of what made your team great in the first place, and now it's gone. Hello mediocrity— unless you nip this in the bud right away. If 20 percent of my team isn't in disagreement on any given topic, I know something is wrong, and I move into antihuddle mode. Unfortunately, once too much huddling is the norm, it is not easy to fix the problem.

What to do? One tactic I use when I see too much huddling is to drop some "bombs." I shake things up. I stop being so agreeable and start stating more objections. Instead of saying yes, I start to say no more often. I become intentionally combative on certain topics where there is total agreement among my team. I create a little conflict to make sure no one becomes too comfortable with the status quo. It wakes people up and shakes them out of their self-satisfaction huddle.

The best business solutions are only developed under relentless scrutiny. If that is not happening on your team anymore, you run the risk of sliding backward toward average. As Zig Ziglar famously said, "Success is not a destination, it's a journey." Stop the huddling and get your team back on track with some friction, arguments, and conflicts.

# Chapter 3

# Manage Power and Fear

So much is currently being written about fear in the corporate environment and how to create "fearless organizations." Most of the time, books and articles on this topic look at examples and surveys from corporate environments where fear exists. Then, they share research about how fear creates a bad culture and leads to negative business results. Finally, they compare these fear-filled environments to those where fear isn't such a big problem and recommend that organizations copy those cultures where fear is managed better. This leads to how-to workshops and seminars led by implementation specialists with five-step systems showing management how to "foster open communication and be respectful when speaking up," "embrace different opinions irrespective of roles," "create a climate of trust," "embody humanity and be socially intelligent," "create a code that, once mentioned, protects employees from negative reactions because the code dictates that nothing said—even criticism—can be held against the employee." You probably know the drill because you've probably attended such sessions throughout your career. It's the corporate way of slapping a little bandage on a gaping wound— and it never changes anything.

If you ask me, it's all nonsense, total BS. Just because somebody tells you *how* to eliminate fear from your culture does not mean that you *can*. Unless the systemic, fundamental problems causing the fear are addressed, all the how-tos in the world won't do the trick. Corporate gimmicks don't address core dysfunctions, which are often the root cause of a fearful culture. It could be a "top down, shut up" hierarchical structure, a lack of trust due to continuous broken promises, tyrannical managers who think they're always right, cowardly leaders who buckle anytime someone higher up wants something, or poor communications processes. I could go on, but you're probably familiar with the long list of corporate maladies.

I love Formula 1 racing, but the current corporate approach is equivalent to trying to teach employees to drive an F1 race car at the Circuit of the Americas in Austin, Texas, in five steps. I can hear the three-hour seminar now: "Step one: Simply put the pedal to the metal at the start. Step two: Finish straight to 210 mph until 50 meters before the left corner at the top of the hill. Step three: Put the brake pedal to 78 percent capacity, turn the steering wheel 46 percent. Step four: Wait until your car has entered the first quarter of the corner, then release the brake. Step five: Gently put the gas foot down again to exit the corner 10 centimeters right of the curb then put the pedal again to the metal!" Okay, you've had your five-step training, are you ready to hit the racetrack and handle a machine that can go from 0 to 200 mph in less than five seconds? It's a ridiculous question to ask, right? Of course the answer is no. But corporate America thinks this type of training could make Formula 1 race car drivers out of all of us in a single afternoon.

As a leader entrusted with people's livelihoods and tasked with building the safest environment possible within your organization, you do need to learn the mechanics and fundamentals of power and fear so you can find creative ways to harness and channel the dynamics they create within your culture. However, it's unlikely that you're going to get that kind of training from within your company. But it's well worth the effort to learn about this topic on your own. A safe environment fortified by trust will help you and your team achieve optimal business results—and in the end, that's the race you're in. If you get it wrong—if your people don't feel safe, and power and fear run amuck—it could send you and your company into a corporate death spiral. Commit to a no-gimmicks approach. Take the time to step back and assess the underlying problems stressing out your people. It's not possible to run an organization that is completely free of fear or anxiety. If you think that's possible, you lack a fundamental understanding of human behavior and the evolutionary value of fear and power. But it is possible to learn how to manage the dynamics fear and power create. And it's certainly possible to adopt behaviors that nurture trust, reduce fear, and manage power. It's not always easy to learn how to encourage these behavioral changes or implement them, but if you give up or ignore the challenge, fear and power will come back to bite you and your team in the butt—and this malady will infect every aspect of your organization and its performance.

## The Fundamentals of Power

Any discussion of fear must start with an exploration of how leaders manage power. According to the Open Education Sociology Dictionary, power is "the ability of an individual, group, or institution to influence or exercise control over other people and achieve their goals despite possible opposition or resistance."[38] When you lead, you are by default in a position of power. By definition, you have more influence and control than your employees. Your power can be used to make decisions, influence others, get projects through the bureaucracy, and so forth. You likely oversee annual reviews, budgets, KPIs, raises, promotions, and who gets roles in highly visible projects. Whether you're comfortable admitting it to yourself or not, that's power. Your power likely intimidates others, even if you don't use intimidation as a leadership tactic. I hope you don't, although many do. Your power touches everything and everyone in your organization. If you've come up through the ranks, you'll have felt the shift over time as your title and authority became more important and senior. Some of your power has been bestowed by management through promotions, and some of your power has been earned by your unique leadership style. Either way, with increased power comes increased responsibility. Throughout this book, we will continually explore the dynamics of your power as a leader. Therefore, it is important to explain a few fundamentals up front.

I've experienced increasing power throughout my professional journey. Over the course of five years, I went from being a marketer with no direct reports to a brand team leader in charge of a few other marketers to a district sales manager in charge of eight people to a department lead overseeing seven subdepartments with about eighty people in the department I was asked to lead. It was a big increase in power over a short period of time. My understanding of power and how to use it had to grow very quickly, as you can imagine. Acceptance of my growing power was the initial step. This might sound easy, but it's not. With power comes not only responsibility but conflict. Most of us manage and use our power for the betterment of our people. However, when you work in a large organization, you'll undoubtedly find others with different views of power who have different, or even less noble, goals, objectives, and agendas. This tension will inevitably lead to conflicts.

According to the classic but still accurate 1959 publication *The Bases of Social Power* [39] [40] by John R. P. French Jr. and Bertram Raven, power can be categorized into a few subcategories:

1.  **Expert power** is based on an individual's expertise in a certain field. This power varies based on the actual or perceived extent of this person's knowledge and results primarily in social influence.

2.  **Referent power** has its basis in the identification of a person or a group with someone else, who this person or group identifies with or desires to be closely associated.

3.  **Legitimate power** arrives when someone enters a certain position within a certain social construct, for example a company. This gives power to the designated leader among the ones who accept this very social construct.

4.  **Reward power** is based on one's ability to reward others. The strength of a person's reward power increases with the magnitude of the reward (perceived or actual) that they are able to bestow.

5.  **Coercive power** involves the power holder's ability to manipulate others by applying pressure to do or believe something, "or else." This power stems from the expectation that there will be a punishment for those who fail to adopt an idea or process or follow through on an assigned task.

In any given situation at any moment in time, all these powers are in play to some degree. When you are a corporate leader, it is very important to be consciously aware of all of them. Your people are well aware that you have the power to punish or reward them. You might not feel this is fair, especially if you consider yourself a fair and just leader, but that's not what matters. What matters is that you understand others have this perception of power and it influences the way they interact with you. There's a reason for that—fear and anxiety. Wherever there is power, you must recognize that there is always fear and anxiety—your own and that of the people you lead. Why? Because in a hierarchical organization, that very power balance is uneven. You have probably heard the saying, "Don't bite the hand that feeds you."

Let's discuss your own fears first. I don't care how courageous you think you are, every leader experiences fear. It's baked into our behaviors as a result of human evolution. You must learn to manage your own fears before you can effectively manage the dynamic of fear in the groups you lead.

When you're studying your own relationship with fear, it's important to remember that you carry a lot of weight on your shoulders as a leader. The higher you go in an organization, the more responsibility you shoulder. It can be a lot. Come to terms with the fact that feeling anxious sometimes comes with the territory. Ignoring negative emotions only makes things worse. At the height of the COVID-19 pandemic, when much of the world was on edge, an August 2021 *Harvard Business Review* article was published by Lauren C. Howe, Jochen I. Menges, and John Monks. Titled "Leaders, Don't Be Afraid to Talk About Your Fears and Anxieties," the article concluded that the best leaders are sharers:

> …sharing negative emotions can lessen their impact on the leader, build empathy between leaders and employees, encourage others to open up about their own negative emotions, and help others recontextualize and overcome those struggles—ultimately boosting morale and performance throughout the organization.

That's definitely a counterintuitive perspective in a business world where leaders are routinely encouraged to be pillars of strength. But times are changing. The pandemic and the "Great Resignation" of 2021 brought to light the fact that humans have become fed up with the state of work. Trust, transparency, authenticity, and integrity have emerged as powerful currencies in the workplace. The days of putting on a brave face are over. It's time to get real with yourself about your relationship with fear. Real power emerges when you have awareness and understanding of those things that trigger fear within you as well as self-awareness around your reactions to those triggers. Once you begin to recognize the signs, you can be more intentional about your behaviors. You can learn to control your evolutionary responses and then teach others to do the same. That's real power at work, don't you think?

## The Evolutionary Role of Fear

Fear and trust can rarely dominate the same corporate culture. As a leader, you must choose one or the other—and the journey begins with self-assessment and personal growth. Fear is always present within you and around you—our human evolution ensures this. The question—and the opportunity—is how you deal with it, because while our evolutionary response to fear can keep us out of harm's way, it can also be counterproductive, even harmful.

In primate social hierarchies—remember, we humans are primates too—fear plays a significant role in maintaining the alpha position, the position of the highest-ranking member in a group. Fear is utilized to reinforce the hierarchy and discourage challengers from attempting to question a leader's authority. While this approach is effective in many primate societies, it is not the only approach to maintaining a balanced system. Pygmy chimpanzees, for example, also known as bonobos, have developed a matriarchal society where social hierarchy is maintained through strong alliances and cooperative behaviors.[41] This has led to a less aggressive, more tolerant, and more flexible social structure. So, there are definitely alternatives to fear and terror, if a leader wishes to create a more congenial culture.

Another evolutionary mechanism that has proven crucial in the preservation and survival of our species is the fight-or-flight response, which helps us detect potential threats and prepare our bodies to react quickly. Evolutionary, neurobiological, and physiological shortcuts in our brain circuitry allow us to ramp up almost instantaneously to meet real or perceived threats. Your muscles flex, your heart beats faster, and your body releases adrenaline, preparing you to either fight or flee at any moment. If the threat is real, your chances of surviving are improved by the fight-or-flight response. If the threat abates or wasn't real, it can take more than a moment to relax—so powerful are these neurobiological and physiological triggers.

In addition to the fight-or-flight response, humans also have a freeze response, a behavioral and physiological reaction in which the body enters a state of immobility or reduced movement, often accompanied by a decrease in heart rate, respiration, and muscle tension. This response is thought to have evolved as a survival mechanism, allowing one to freeze and become less noticeable or threatening to a predator or while in a dangerous situation. In modern times, when one is much less likely to meet a saber-toothed tiger at the office, the freeze response can occur in various stressful or threatening situations. It may be triggered by a perception of helplessness or the belief that there's no way out of a situation. A freeze response can be elicited by witnessing a traumatic event, experiencing a sudden threat, or being confronted with overwhelming stressors. Some people may have a tendency to freeze more readily or frequently, while others may exhibit a fight-or-flight response.

Who hasn't been in a professional situation where a higher-up verbally attacked you and you froze because you didn't know how to react? It happens every day.

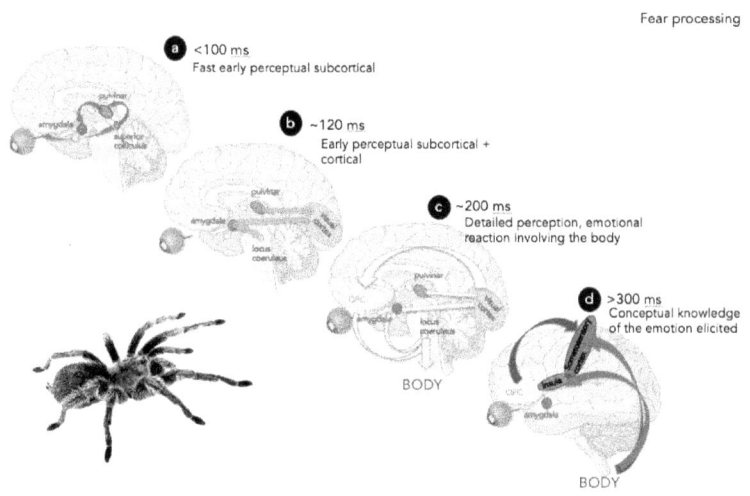

Fear processing

**a** <100 ms
Fast early perceptual subcortical

**b** ~120 ms
Early perceptual subcortical + cortical

**c** ~200 ms
Detailed perception, emotional reaction involving the body

**d** >300 ms
Conceptual knowledge of the emotion elicited

BODY

BODY

Partly generated with biorender

*Figure 1: Thanks to evolution, a cascade of events happens very rapidly in our brains when we encounter a threatening stimulus. First, in less than one-tenth of a second, archaic regions of the brain, like the subcortical system, process the presence of the threat and activate the amygdala. It then takes about twenty milliseconds for the amygdala to put the rest of the brain on alert, enhancing the capacities of the visual cortex and activating a region of the brain known as the locus coeruleus, which releases the stress neurotransmitter norepinephrine. By two hundred milliseconds, the entire brain is on high alert, and we start to have an emotional reaction to the stimulus. It takes more than three hundred milliseconds for the brain's frontal lobes to start sorting through the emotions that have been triggered. Partly generated with BioRender.*

As explained in figure 1, these are all involuntary responses. No one can stop the body's reactions or escape nature's built-in responses to fears and threats. We can only learn to be more aware and manage them. Nouchine Hadjikhani, MD, PhD, Director of Neurolimbic Research at Harvard Medical School, says:

It's very reasonable to hypothesize that fear-related behaviors, such as freezing or avoidance, may still be influenced by our evolutionary neurobiological/physiological circuitry. When facing a verbally threatening or intimidating situation, such as dealing with a "mean" boss, the brain may activate similar fear-related circuits as it would in the presence of a physical threat. The amygdala, for example, plays a central role in evaluating emotional significance, including fear, and it could be activated in response to a perceived threat from an authority figure. The danger with this is that the trigger of physiological behaviors that are associated with this reaction is potentially harmful for the body over time. Renowned primatologist Robert Sapolsky has written a great book on this topic, called *Why Zebras Don't Get Ulcers*.[42]

The bottom line to all of this is that fear isn't something we can just wish away or pretend we don't experience. You are not a fearless superhero, and pretending you are is not good for your well-being or the well-being of your people. There is no getting around fear, even if it makes you uncomfortable. So, you need to deal with it, otherwise you won't be able to build a culture of trust where people feel as safe as possible. You know you need this type of environment to achieve optimal business results, so it's time to stare fear in the face. Showing your people that you are aware of the power imbalance and the fears associated with it means your people feel understood. Once you demonstrate that you're not going to take advantage of this imbalance, you'll earn their increasing trust. That's why recognizing and properly managing power and fear is so important—and the journey starts with managing your own relationship with power and fear first.

## Create a Safe Environment

The November 2020 *Journal of Psychiatric Research* report,[43] *Trends in Anxiety Among Adults in the United States, 2008–2018*, shared this unsettling finding: anxiety "has broadly increased among adults in the US over the past decade . . . consistently across racial/ethnic, gender and income subgroups . . ." The American Psychological Association (APA) also signaled increasing stress levels in its annual report, *Stress in America*.[44] Their 2017 edition cited the three most common sources of stress as: (1) the future of the nation (63 percent); (2) money (62 percent); and (3) work (61 percent). And these findings were from *before* the global COVID-19 pandemic, which added significantly more stress to our lives. In 2020, in the middle of the pandemic, the APA issued a warning: we are facing a national mental health crisis that could yield serious health and social consequences for years to come. A year later, that stress and anxiety would hit the workplace hard. By November 2021, the nation's "quit rate" had reached a twenty-year high. One study concluded: "One of the main reasons believed to underlie the Great Resignation is prolonged distress, or *burnout*.[45] Burnout refers to a state of being depleted of physical and emotional energy and reflects a chronic stress syndrome."[46]

As a leader in the twenty-first century, you must face the fact that stress, fear, and anxiety have a profound impact on every aspect of the modern workplace, including productivity, retention, innovation, strategy, and everything else you can think of. It's one reason soft skills like empathy, emotional intelligence, situational and self-awareness, emotional control, and strong communication and listening skills have become increasingly important for leaders. If you want to build and execute strategy effectively in today's workplace, you must learn these skills, because whether you realize it or not stress, fear, and anxiety are having a profound impact on your team's dynamics, decision-making, and behaviors. I don't know about you, but I find these increasing levels of stress, fear, and anxiety quite unsettling, and I certainly don't take them lightly. If there is one thing that keeps me up a night in a business context, it's the well-being of my team members, colleagues, and direct reports. As a leader, you are responsible for them. As we've discussed several times in this book—because it is so important—you need to create a safe environment so your people can cope with all the pressures and uncertainties that lead to the abovementioned negative dynamics. If you get it right, you might be able to create an "island" of happiness and collegiality for your people. I've seen this happen and was part of some groups that were able to achieve this. It's not easy, but it is possible. In a minute, we'll dive into how I believe you can get there. But before we do, let's define our lexicon. While stress, fear, and anxiety might often occur together, the terms are not interchangeable. All three interact with one another and can be the cause and consequence of the others.

> **Stress**, as defined by the World Health Organization, is "a state of worry or mental tension caused by a difficult situation. Stress is a natural human response that prompts us to address challenges and threats in our lives. Everyone experiences stress to some degree . . .[47] Stress affects both the mind and the body. A little bit of stress is good and can help us perform daily activities. Too much stress can cause physical and mental health problems." Think about the difference between speaking in front of a crowd, a situation where a little stress might improve your performance, versus the stress of living in poverty, a permanent and debilitating stress that negatively impacts the quality of a person's life.

> **Fear** is an intense, biological response to an immediate danger. If you're hiking and see a mountain lion or a bear, you are afraid and take quick action to protect yourself. As we've discussed, fear is an important evolutionary survival mechanism that has kept our species alive.

> **Anxiety**, on the other hand, is defined by the APA (American Psychological Association) as: "an emotion characterized by feelings of tension, worried thoughts, and physical changes

like increased blood pressure . . . Anxiety is not the same as fear . . . Anxiety is considered a future-oriented, long-acting response broadly focused on a diffuse threat, whereas fear is an appropriate, present-oriented, and short-lived response to a clearly identifiable and specific threat."[48] Evolutionary researchers theorize that in ancient times, anxiety made us more cautious, which was advantageous in an environment with many natural predators and threats. The trait was passed down because it helped us survive. Today, however, with fewer threats and more command over our environment, anxiety persists as a human coping mechanism. And, like other evolutionary traits and biases, it now plays a different and often disruptive role in our lives. According to the National Institute of Health, about 31 percent of the US population experiences an anxiety disorder at some time in their lives, so a lot of people are struggling with the effects of this genetic characteristic.[49]

Let's take a moment to return to the opening message of this book: know thyself. As a leader, if you're not self-aware enough to address how stress, fear, and anxiety might be clouding your own judgement and shaping your own negative behaviors, you might actually be contributing to the anxiety problem at your workplace. According to an April 2023 article in *Forbes*, "The stress felt by managers can cascade to employees, impacting well-being, retention, and performance. *Harvard Business Review* finds managers can trigger anxiety in their employers through unusual or erratic actions, emotional volatility, excessive pessimism, and ignoring people's emotions. Managers that withdraw or are more 'hot-headed' have teams that are 62 percent more likely to leave their jobs and 56 percent more likely to stop participating."[50] If you don't think this type of scenario negatively impacts the creation, implementation, and adoption of important strategies, you're deluding yourself. Do the work as an individual first. Then, do the work as a team. Explore how stress, fear, and anxiety are impacting your leadership, your people, and your culture. Address the problems you uncover. I have experienced firsthand the type of havoc that uneducated and reckless leaders can unleash in the workplace. I have seen employees not sleeping well for weeks before big presentations. I have witnessed irresponsible leaders send last-minute weekend requests to entire teams. These requests killed family and relaxation time, which is exactly what stressed-out employees need to rejuvenate. I have watched employees literally shaking in fear, sometimes even drugging themselves, before entering the boardroom or executive meeting. This should not be acceptable, but in many corporate cultures, it is. Stress, fear, and anxiety are ever-more prevalent in the work environment. Put simply, failing to address what's causing this uptick is not an option anymore.

So, let's revisit one of the most important questions I aim to answer in this book: How can leaders create a safe environment in which everyone can benefit from our evolutionary heritage instead of falling victim to it? We've already established you cannot create work environments that eliminate fear, stress, and anxiety altogether. Human evolution has made this impossible. What you can do, though, is create a safe environment that recognizes the human condition and helps people deal with it. If you can accomplish this at an individual and team level, you're setting everyone up for more productivity, authentic collaboration, better communication, accelerated innovation, and ultimately higher achievement.

Unfortunately, safe environments are the exception, not the norm. And if you're stepping into a leadership position for the first time, chances are you haven't fully acknowledged or addressed your own stressors, anxieties, and fears. This means you're not in an ideal position to confront the dynamics of fear, stress, and anxiety in your team. As we discussed earlier in the book, whether you like it or not, your position of power is part of this dynamic. Leaders will always be the foundation (or the undoing) of a safe environment. So first and foremost, do the hard personal work to become more self-aware and intentional in what you say and do.

If you're a more seasoned leader and are asked to lead a new team, you'll probably have to acknowledge and fix what was broken in the past. This is a crucial first step before people start to feel safe again—even if you're doing everything right as the new person at the helm.

If you've been in the same leadership position for a while, there's a chance you've become blind to what's broken. Before you can create a safer environment, you'll have to open your eyes to what needs fixing. All of this is to say that you're never going to walk into a room full of people you've been asked to lead and find a safe environment waiting for you. A sense of safety, our evolution tells us, is ever-shifting. Even when it is built over time, it can be easily shattered by a mistake. It takes time, hard work, and discipline to build and maintain a safe environment, so you need a long-term mindset.

What are some crucial next steps to build a safe environment that allows your team to thrive and achieve more together?

## Make Safety a Team Goal

Effective leaders understand that organically created and shared goals and responsibilities are always more effective and more readily adopted than corporate commands that come down from on high. That's why when it comes to creating a safe environment for your people, you need to involve them in the process. They need to help define what a safe culture looks like and how it is monitored. They need to help set up the processes to put this new environment in place and make sure it sticks—and hopefully continues to evolve and get stronger.

## Be Vulnerable

As I've mentioned several times throughout this book, trust is a powerful currency. And people tend to trust people who admit they don't know everything and admit to their mistakes. Allow yourself to be vulnerable sometimes—and I don't mean to *say* you're vulnerable, I mean to actually *be* vulnerable. Paying lip service to this characteristic will backfire. However, being authentically vulnerable from time to time will demonstrate through actual behavior that you define power differently than what your people have experienced before. It shows your team that power and vulnerability can coexist, and it gives them permission to be vulnerable too. This is a powerful practice to build trust, which is foundational for all safe environments. Sometimes, when I mention that leaders should show they are vulnerable, I'm asked, "How can I do this?" The answer is simple: just be transparent. We *are* all vulnerable at times, so when those moments hit, don't try to hide your vulnerability—show it! And if you can't, it's beneficial to work on your self-confidence.

## Admit Mistakes

Self-confident leaders are not afraid to admit when they are wrong. They do so freely, openly, and publicly. In other words, they accept that they screwed up. They own it! They are usually very comfortable in their own skin, and they understand that everyone messes up. To them, a mistake is an opportunity to learn and get better. Imagine the example, and the tone, this sets for a team. It gives them permission to make mistakes, learn, and improve. This creates a safe environment for innovative thinking and action, which can have a very positive impact on performance. Never underestimate the power of these soft skills in building a strong, high-performance culture. Second, truly self-confident and vulnerable leaders encourage honest feedback from others and receive it stoically. No matter how negative the feedback is and how much it hurts, never dare to justify or explain yourself. When your team is setting up the parameters for the safe environment they want to create, a strong feedback process should be created. It might sometimes feel uncomfortable, but it's key to any safe environment. You can't improve as a leader if you don't know how others see you or are impacted by your ideas, processes, and behaviors. Be open to the ongoing professional and personal growth this feedback will provide.

## Mind Your Own Narcissism

We are all narcissists to some degree—some more than others. The ego is an important part of our evolution, as the ability to understand ourselves as individuals that are separate from our environment is one of the defining factors that make humans human. Yet, the very ego that plays a positive role in getting people into leadership positions can become destructive if it starts to dominate their behavior. If that happens, we become self-absorbed narcissists. Sometime stress, anxiety, or fear get the better of us, and we get defensive and let our egos cloud our thoughts. We've all been there. We think someone wants our job and start guarding our territory to the detriment of collaboration. That's narcissistic. Or something isn't working as expected and we become afraid that we'll be blamed, so instead of confronting the issue, we hide it so we don't look bad. Or we feel belittled because someone has spoken out against us or our ideas. We feel the urge to explain and defend ourselves. Or we "have to" speak up because someone said something important and we need to "second" that or "add" to it or "build" on it to hear ourselves speak while nothing is said. All of this is our ego taking control and making us act like a narcissist. As a leader, it can be easy to slip into these counterproductive behaviors. Since a person's ego is often the key driver in their professional rise to power, successful professionals tend to trust their egos. But when the going gets tough, that trust in the ego can backfire and allow narcissism to creep in. Narcissists are not capable of genuine vulnerability. They cannot foster trust or muster up empathy. Make sure to keep your ego in check for the good of yourself and your team.

## Remember Stress, Fear, and Anxiety Are Contagious

Our bodies have a remarkable ability to convey and pick up on emotions—and stress, fear, and anxiety are no exception. We know that those are contagious and that this contagion spreads through body language. Using functional brain imaging, science can demonstrate that observing bodies expressing fear without seeing any facial expression still trigger the same circuitry as that activated by stimuli eliciting fear, and that the body gets prepared to act accordingly. So, if you are afraid, it will consciously or unconsciously elicit fear in those around you, redirecting energy away from productivity and into a state of self-preservation, which is typically not a productive state of mind. This is one more reason that, as leaders, we need to try to manage and ideally tame our fears.

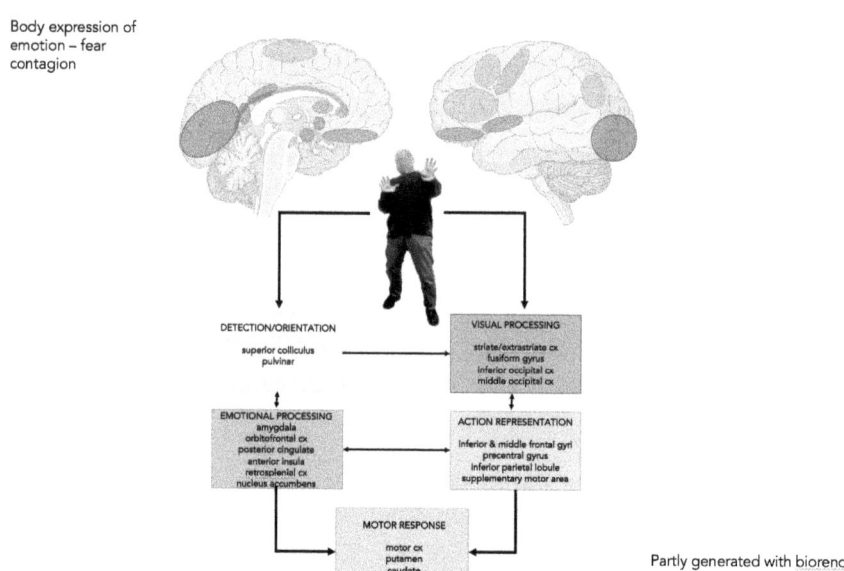

*Figure 2: An illustration based on a neuroimaging study about how fear fosters flight. Researchers Beatrice de Gelder, Josh Snyder, Doug Greve, George Gerard, and Nouchine Hadjikhani explored a mechanism for contagious fear by showing how the brain reacts when it sees body expression of emotion without clues from facial expression. Two major things happen when observing an emotion in another person. First, our brain mirrors and tries to understand and feel what the other person is experiencing. This is the basis of human empathy. Second, if we're observing someone showing signs of fear, our brain activity*

*increases in areas linked to our evolutionary fight-or-flight response. When this happens, our body language starts to convey the emotions we are observing in another person.[51] Partly generated with BioRender.*

In a group, this chain reaction can get out of hand. That's why your body language matters big-time as a leader. You are the person everyone is watching. You are the barometer of how things are going. Everyone is constantly observing your "read" on things. Albert Mehrabian, a professor emeritus of psychology at the University of California, Los Angeles, created the 7-38-55 Rule, a communication model that says that only 7 percent of the communication of feelings and attitudes is conveyed through the words we speak, while 38 percent takes place through tone and voice, and the remaining 55 percent of communication is through body language.[52] Mehrabian's findings suggest strongly that leaders need to watch their body language even more closely than what they say to their employees. How a leader walks out of a difficult meeting or controversial budget discussion is more important than how the leader recounts the meeting to his or her people. If your shoulders are hanging and you bypass your usual stop at the coffee machine because you don't want to talk about it, your folks will start to worry. They will wonder what's going on. They'll start commenting that the boss is behaving oddly, to see if others agree. They'll start to worry that bad news is coming. Rumors will start swirling and tensions will start building. Don't let this happen. Don't let your body tell a story to your team that you don't want to tell. Your body speaks a very specific and powerful language, so make sure the narrative it is telling aligns with the one you're sharing verbally with your people.

Today's leaders must understand the human condition, which includes uncertainty, stress, fear, and anxiety. How these emotions are handled will have a profound impact on productivity, retention, innovation, strategy, and everything else. If you want to build and execute strategy effectively in today's competitive and fast-moving marketplace, you must master empathy, emotional intelligence, situational and self-awareness, emotional control, strong communi-cation, and listening skills. Don't underestimate the power of these "soft skills." They have a major impact on performance. While it's easy as a leader to get caught up in bottom-line metrics, it's the well-being of your team that matters most. If you can keep this at the forefront of your leadership philosophy, in the good times and bad, you and your team will ultimately come out on top. Always remember, as business leader, you don't really lead the business. You lead the people who do the business!

# Chapter 4

# Lead Like You Want
# to Be Led

We started with a discussion about how to lead yourself, then moved on to the rules of team building. Now it's time to think about leading the way you want to be led. Copy everything you liked about the leadership strategies from successful teams you were on and avoid everything you disliked from unsuccessful or toxic teams. It's that simple. In this chapter, we'll call out some of the top behaviors of effective leadership. If you apply these behaviors, your chances for a successful leadership journey will increase dramatically.

# Walk Your Talk

Do you embody the behaviors you expect from your team? I mean really. It is not enough to adopt the guidelines you set for others once or twice a week. I'm talking about walking your talk 24/7. Do you know your core values and live by them? If not, you can't expect others to do what you are not willing to do yourself. If you want your people to be quick and nimble, you must be quick and nimble. Among other things, this means you can't let emails sit in your inbox for days at a time if you expect your people to respond within hours. That's hypocrisy! People don't trust or give their best to hypocrites; they just make fun of them. Make sure you're willing to walk your talk if you want to be an effective leader.

Here are a few examples of how walking your talk looks in the real world. If you genuinely want your people to have a decent work-life balance, but you stay in the office until 8:00 p.m. every night, your team will notice, and your excuses about why you can't go home won't hold water with your team. If you want your people to step in and get their hands dirty on important projects, you've got to be willing to take a chunk of that work too. If you want your people to ensure all stakeholders are briefed before big meetings, make sure you always have your peers on board. If you want to establish a competitive and winning culture for your team, make sure you yourself take it personally when the competitor takes away a chunk of your business. If you want your team to stay fit, don't be lazy yourself. Instead, organize a charity 10k race you can all participate in.

You're smart, and I know you get my point. But when you're tired and juggling too much, it's easy to say, "Just do it!" to your team. It's not so easy to walk your talk 24/7. However, just because it's hard doesn't mean you can skip it. Whatever culture you want to establish, you need live and breathe it yourself first. Only then will your people follow. You can't build a high-performance team unless you walk your talk.

# Know Your People

You must know your people. This leadership truth cannot be taught or faked; it must come from within—from the work you do to become the best leader you can be. If you are lucky enough to be asked to step up and lead a group of human beings, it is assumed you'll bring your best self to the job. Unfortunately, too many "leaders" treat their people like homogenous robots whose only purpose is to meet targets and achieve goals. Some "leaders" don't even bother to know their people's names—even after being in the job for months. How inspiring! People are not robots! The team you are leading is made up of a diverse group of individuals. They all might be working toward a common goal, but as we've discussed, they all have different drivers, aspirations, interests, and personalities. While one individual might be driven by personal interactions with the company's customers and prospects, another might be inspired by the intellectual challenge of learning the sophisticated subject matter he or she is required to master. A third individual might be driven by the opportunity to advance in the company, and a fourth by the work-life balance the job allows. I could go on forever with these real-world examples of top performers I've had the honor of working with in my many leadership roles.

Get to know all the unique people on your team. Though everyone comes together on a high-performing team to overcome challenges and meet or exceed shared goals, you can only unlock the individual potential of your team if you know each member. While conversation will be focused on KPIs and the approach to achieve these KPIs, the discussion can be customized based on what you know about each team member's drivers, interests, and aspirations. You can tailor your approach, communication style, and even the topics you cover. This leads to more meaningful and effective conversations. In my early years as a professional, I didn't do this. I tried to talk with everyone in the same way, to keep them all focused on the essentials. Over time, my experience taught me the opposite was more effective. Leaving room for individuality leads to better, more creative, less additive, and more synergistic outcomes.

This customized, individualized approach should guide all your team interactions. If you don't speak to people in a language they understand, you might as well be speaking a foreign language. It won't translate. Conversely, if you get it right and you speak directly to what matters to someone, greatness can and will happen. Not only will each member perform to his or her full potential, but you'll unlock the unique energy that can only be discovered and tapped when all the individuals on your team feel valued and appreciated for their unique skills, interests, and contributions. When a team like that comes together—in no small part because the leader of that team has genuinely gotten to know his or her people—it unleashes the immense and exponential power of human potential.

## Foster Individual Development from Day One

Having established that human behavior is driven by evolutionary forces that benefit individual fitness, leaders have a choice. They can either lean into the opportunity this presents or ignore it—and if they choose the latter, they do so at their own peril (for all the reasons we've already mentioned in previous sections of this chapter). The best way to connect human self-interest to team building is to be a partner to your team members. This means you start working with your people from day one on their development plan. What are their personal and professional goals? What do they want to achieve in the short term and down the road in their career? It may be the employee's responsibility to create these goals, but it is the leader's responsibility to guide this process and help the employee shape and execute their development plan. In fact, as a leader, you should schedule certain dates and times on your calendar when you reach out proactively to schedule employee-development-plan conversations. These sessions should be designed to provide feedback and guidance as well as help the individual address potential gaps and roadblocks on their road map to achieving their goals.

There's a reason, I titled this chapter "Lead How You Want to Be Led." Put yourself in the employee's mindset for a moment. Would you like to be managed by a leader who never brings up your career goals? Someone who dismisses your career development as an after-thought and only pays it lip service? Someone who delegates your career development to the human resources department? Or would you prefer to be part of a team lead by someone who proactively schedules time to talk with you about your career aspirations and works with you consistently to achieve your personal goals? I think we all know the answer. If you act like the first leader, you clearly don't understand what drives human behavior, and you're missing out on a huge opportunity to nurture trust and gain the respect of your team members. Don't make this mistake. Build an environment in which the development of your people is left, right, and center from day one. And always remember that the best way to get better as leader is to make your people better.

## Challenge and Be Challenged

In my experience, the best solutions come from intense, sometimes even controversial, discussions among team members. I've also seen great ideas emerge after working through a conflict as a team. As I mentioned earlier in the book, I welcome a little friction, because that's where change, growth, and innovation start. If I'm not seeing these types of scenarios, or if I'm seeing complacency, I'm inclined to ignite a controversy and create some friction. A well-timed and properly managed conflict can be an effective tool. But there's a caveat . . .

If you like to start conflicts occasionally, you also need to be willing to have the occasional conflict dropped on you. That's right, if you challenge your team, they need to be able to challenge you right back. The rules of the game must apply to everyone. You cannot play the leader card when the going gets tough. This might seem obvious, but you would be surprised by how many leaders have a sense of entitlement and think they should be above the rules they set for their team. Big mistake.

I have always sought to be challenged by others. I have always encouraged my teams to provide me with feedback. When they do, I thank them for their opinions, even when they are tough to hear. I can honestly say that some of the biggest lessons I've learned in my professional life have happened when direct reports told me in very straight language what I did or did not do well or what I need to do differently. I've been told people appreciated this about me. I've also been told by too many people that they have not experienced this type of open, two-way communication with their boss before. These people are especially appreciative of my management style. In fact, for some, the act of giving feedback to their boss is so new, they apologize to me as they share their opinions. How crazy and alarming is this?

If you build an environment in which people do not speak up because they think they might insult you, you have failed as a leader. Sadly, you will not learn as much as you could have, and you will not achieve optimal outcomes, because your search for the best solutions is being choked by an environment lacking in any frank, two-way questioning and discussion. You've created a team culture where there's no friction, which means you have stifled your team's creative energy and ability to effectively problem solve and innovate.

Build an environment that is safe for friction, dissent, and candor—an environment in which everyone can be challenged, including you. If you want to become a leader who can drive important and ongoing transformation in your organization, you need to be able to build this type of environment. The hallmark of transformation is to constantly challenge the status quo, and you can only do this if you create an open, honest culture where conflicting ideas and viewpoints are openly considered. Embrace the friction. Challenge and be challenged!

## Never Ask Your People to Collect Wood

*"If you want to build a ship, do not drum up people to collect wood and do not assign them tasks and work, but rather teach them to long for the endless immensity of the sea."* Those are the famous translated words of the French aristocrat, writer, and aviator Antoine de Saint-Exupéry, most prominently known for his bestselling novel *The Little Prince*.[53] Monsieur Saint-Exupéry beautifully expressed an extremely important leadership principle: show your people their higher purpose.

Be honest, what gets you out of bed every morning aren't the meetings on your calendar, the slide presentation you must finish, or the sales goals your team must meet this quarter. What gets all of us out of bed is the higher purpose of our work. If you are leading with slogans like, "We are here to increase our market share," or "We are in the business of completing this project on time and under budget," then you have already lost the interest of your people. If these are the only things you're asking your people to achieve, it is only a matter of time before your competitors start contacting your top performers and offering them more money. You shouldn't be surprised when they are gone in a heartbeat. Why? Because you failed to inspire and lead them toward their higher purpose. Every day, you must remind your people why their work is important. Higher purpose comes in many shapes and forms. Sometimes it's external— for example, achieving something remarkable like President John F. Kennedy's historic mission to put a man on the moon, which ignited a nation and came true despite tremendous odds. In 1962, when JFK was visiting the NASA space center, he noticed a janitor carrying a broom. The president walked over to him and introduced himself.

"Hi, I'm John Kennedy. What are you doing?" he asked, extending his hand.

"Well, Mr. President," the janitor responded, "I'm helping put a man on the moon."

This was how deeply ingrained NASA's mission was within the organization. Other times, higher purpose is internal, like safeguarding a company's legacy, brand, reputation, or mission. What would Amazon be without its stellar reputation for customer service. What would Disney be without the magic?

Of course, the highest purpose of all is doing good for others.

When the manager at a home construction company reminds his people that they're not just building houses but providing *homes* for hundreds of families, he shifts his team's perspective. When the sales director at a biopharmaceutical business reminds her people that they aren't just selling medications but rather advancing science for patients in need, she creates strong inspiration for her team. Remember from discussions in earlier chapters that we humans are wired to help others because it is in our own self-interest. From our unique evolution, we have learned that reciprocal altruism is one of the strongest evolutionary drivers, because we need others so we and our offspring can survive and thrive. A big part of our entire cultural heritage is built around this concept and passed on from generation to generation. It's how we *Homo sapiens*—despite being weak, slow, and mostly unarmed—are still flourishing as a species. We have remarkable brains that allow us to collaborate and mutually help one another.

Without knowing it, our home construction manager and biopharmaceutical sales director are invoking reciprocal altruism. They have shown their people why their work matters and how it helps others in need of a home or a medical treatment. The importance of doing good for others is so ingrained in our human psyche that our brains have created neurochemical shortcuts to encourage us to behave in this way. These shortcuts literally make it feel good to do good for others.

So, if you want your people to get out of bed every day to climb that next mountain at work, show them their higher purpose—how they are doing good for others. If you can do this authentically and meaningfully, you will unlock potent energy. You will tap into one of the most powerful and longest-standing of humanity's evolutionary drivers. This is not an exaggeration. And, if you can infuse this higher purpose into your culture and strategy, you will become practically invincible—and your people and teams will be unstoppable!

## Everyone Is a Champion

*One of the biggest lessons I've learned as a leader is that I do not have to know everything or be the best at everything. As a young professional, I tried so hard to be the smartest and the best. I failed, of course. How could I not? Instead of learning from my coworkers and direct reports by valuing their unique skills and experience, I felt threatened. If someone understood a concept more quickly or was more experienced with something, my insecurities took over. I was always running in circles trying to catch up and learn everything. I now understand this isn't possible, or wise. No one can know everything or be the best at everything. We all have strengths and weaknesses based on our unique experiences, capabilities, and skills.*

*Reflecting on these early career mistakes now always makes me smile and shake my head. If only I could have told my younger self, "Don't waste your time, Nicolas. Relax! You don't need to know everything to be a successful leader." Today, as a senior leader with many years* of experience and much more professional confidence, my approach is completely different. I actively pursue talented people who can expertly cover my blind spots. I seek out those who can close skills and experience gaps on my teams. Yes, these people are smarter than me and better than me in certain areas, and that's a good thing. I know now that no one can be a champion of everything, but everyone can be a champion of something! That's a life-changing realization. As a leader, it allows me to build  high-performing teams instead of wasting time trying to do and be better than everyone else. I get to shape and lead teams composed of talented people who each have unique backgrounds, experiences, and areas of expertise. This is a much more efficient, less stressful, and more successful way to lead.

I call members of my team subject matter experts (SME)—a title that shows them they are highly valued and respected. Being known as an SME nurtures self-esteem. This, in turn, means my people have a higher level of commitment, a better attitude, and more job satisfaction. Everyone on your team should be called an expert in their particular area of expertise. The person's skill might not be immediately obvious, but I guarantee that if you take the time to identify each person on your team as an SME in something, your group's true potential will start to reveal itself.

On my teams, I've named SMEs in contracting, compliance, sales, marketing, and customer relations, to name just a few. Sometimes the area of expertise isn't even considered a business skill. Maybe one of your team members coaches teen sports and understands motivation better than others. Perhaps there's an artist on your team who can spruce up governance or leadership presentations. If you can identify these special talents in your group, then—and only then—will you be able to fully leverage your group's unique talent profile.

One of my good friends is a conductor in Europe. Having led many of the world's most famous orchestras, he once told me that every *performance is different—even when the music is the same. He explained that each musician plays with unique style and skill, and the distinctive mix of individuals with any given orchestra changes the overall sound of the performance. He said he loved this aspect of his job. He enjoyed the unexpected. I love it too. It shows how individual talents contribute to the performance of the whole, often with amazing and surprising results. If you allow the individuals on your team to shine and showcase their unique talents—and if you nurture those talents instead of trying to acquire all those talents yourself—the outcome will be better than you might imagine. Great leaders acknowledge this truth. They develop their team's distinctive strengths, so they can orchestrate and enjoy a unique performance with every new team and project.*

## Lead Soft, Manage Hard

Being a strong leader requires an enormous number of soft skills. Like a spider, you must be sensitive to even the smallest vibrations in your web. You must be able to read individuals and teams and *feel* their dynamics. You must learn what inspires them, annoys them, scares them, and so forth.

These soft skills are teachable but only to those who are open to learning and who work to become better versions of themselves every day. These types of people realize that perfect leadership can never be achieved and that only the journey of continuous self-improvement can be optimized. Your ability to be highly in tune with your team has a lot to do with your personal makeup—like how interested you are in others, your emotional intelligence, your communication style, your sensitivity, and your ability to navigate various social groups. I have seen fantastic managers who never became great leaders because they did not have, develop, or hone their soft skills. They were never able to build a winning culture where people didn't simply do their jobs but rather tried to change the world for the better every day. Without soft skills, these managers could not build an environment in which people could be utmost fearless and feel empowered to do whatever it might take to make the impossible possible.

But let's imagine you have all the finely tuned soft skills you need to shape a high-performing culture. That's quite an achievement, and you should pat yourself on the back. But you need more to maintain success. To manage people effectively, you also need hard skills. This means you manage based on facts, objective measurements, agreed-upon KPIs, and defined targets. If there is one truism I have learned in my career, it is this: numbers should guide (not determine) every decision you make as a leader. Numbers make you fearless. You can justify *everything* with numbers—the good, the bad, and the ugly. Therefore, you need to *know* your numbers better than anyone else. Here are my three top tips when it comes to numbers.

## Your People Must Understand the Numbers

Perhaps you've experienced something like I experienced midcareer: I was working as part of a team that was charged with an important business and cultural transformation. The stakes were enormous. We had to instigate this change within a corporate culture where no one trusted anyone. It took us many months, but through talking and listening, we were able to establish a very low level of trust between the new leadership team and the concerned teams. These employees had been used to working alone, figuring everything out by themselves in silos, and not sharing, because it was the safest and most successful way to survive in the toxic corporate culture that my team inherited. Of course, as we shaped this massive transformation, we also had to keep the company growing. At the time, it was one of the biggest challenges I had faced in my career.

In order to show the cautious individuals in this department what a successful team looked like, we initially focused on celebrating the critical business KPIs. We partnered with the most successful employees, did our utmost to ensure they understood and embraced our mission, and simply and genuinely asked them for help. But despite our successful bridge-building efforts, there was a disconnect. While personal and strategic conversations improved, it was still extremely difficult to discuss business matters at a tactical or local level. To find the source of this disconnect, we established small local business reviews where most of the agenda was left to the employees. These reviews were done in the towns and cities where the teams were located. Instead of the teams traveling to headquarters, as they had in the past, management was asked to travel to the teams. This played out very well and was an even bigger win with the employees than any of us had expected. But that was only the first surprise. The second was a true shocker, and it was around the numbers. In our first meeting, I walked to a flip chart and drew a simple market share versus market size matrix. Within minutes, it was clear that even the most successful employees in attendance had no idea what these numbers meant to the company's success. In fact, no one had ever asked anyone on these teams about their understanding of any of the KPIs they were asked to achieve, nor had they explained their importance in achieving the company's strategic goals or trained them on how to achieve these KPIs. It became painfully obvious that it was not possible to get the tactical and executional part of the business moving in the right direction because the teams being asked to execute did not understand the KPIs with which their success was measured.

Think about the implications of this for a moment. Not only were the teams being guided by KPIs they did not understand, but their fundamental lack of understanding had negatively impacted the trust between the teams and their management. How could it not? Performance evaluations and bonus payouts were based on KPIs the employees didn't even understand—and this had been going on for *years*!

Once we had identified the problem, the fix was pretty simple: a business intelligence campaign was started, team champions were defined, and trainings were held to educate everyone on the KPIs. Just a few months later, the teams did their own sophisticated analysis of their territories, which enabled them to draw mind-blowing conclusions that resulted in best-in-class resource allocation, competitive intelligence, and related mitigation strategies.

The result for me was that in every assignment thereafter, I made sure *everyone* fully understood the critical numbers. I did this through proactive conversations and Q&A sessions. Sometimes, teams needed personal coaching or tutorials; other times, they needed trainings across functions and departments. Whatever it took, I made it happen, because I had seen firsthand what happens when people don't understand the numbers.

Even if you feel confident your team understands your organization's critical numbers, my advice is this: randomly pick a few members out of your team and ask them to answer the questions below.

- What are the most important criteria and KPIs that demonstrate whether our business is flourishing or scrambling, and how do those criteria interact?
- What are the criteria upon which your performance evaluation is based?
- How are these criteria calculated to measure your performance?

If they all give you the right and same answer without blinking, you are in a great spot. If not, you are likely setting yourself and everyone else up for an unpleasant surprise. It's time to start educating everyone—and fast!

## Your Numbers Must Tell Your Story

Numbers should inform decisions. They provide clarity. They offer guardrails when navigating new territories. They can orientate you in unsettling times. They can replace fear with courage. But numbers alone are not enough. People do not buy numbers; they buy stories. Remember, whether you are presenting to your management team or your people, you are always selling something—and stories are the best sales tools. This means your numbers must tell a story. If the story is good, your audience will buy in.

To build a high-performance culture, you must create number-guided stories that engage, empower, inspire, and help your team understand why and how their performance could be better. There is *always* room for improvement, even with successful teams. Start by asking your frontline people for the numbers because they are the people living and breathing them. Then, interpret those numbers and develop your stories based on what those numbers are telling you. It doesn't matter whether your team is struggling with or crushing the numbers, you must be specific—you can never be general in your number storytelling. No one can learn anything from phrases like, "Market share is great, keep going," or "Market share sucks, up your hit rate." Your stories must be detailed, relatable, and provide a clear, numbers-driven road map showing everyone how to get to the next level.

When talking to management, always remember that you depend on these people to provide resources and salaries for your team. You *need* their support, so they must buy into your stories as well. When telling a success story, it should be the same as the one you told your team—only with a different tone. Adapt to your audience. CFOs and COOs usually prefer facts and numbers over passion and emotions. Conversely, when you have to explain why results were below expectations, craft your story first, then substantiate it with the numbers. Why? Because you need to manage your management.

Your story must explain why you are not there yet or why you need more time, resources, or both. Your story might even need to explain why you and your team need a different goal put in place in order to be successful. If you know your numbers and have them at your fingertips, you will be able to substantiate your story. Perhaps targets were missed because of an "unexpected" slowdown in market growth, loss of exclusivity, or a new competitor. We all know the drill for these "unexpected" events: the company has been preparing for five years, but nobody took the threat seriously, and now there's no plan to deal with the problem as it actually hits. Your numbers will explain these "unexpected" events.

You also need a solid story, because it is only a matter of time before someone comes after you. How often have you seen budget reviews where one department goes after an underperforming unit's resources? How often have you seen performance reviews where those same people try to get better ratings for their people by putting down your people? Expressing why this is unfair won't help. It also won't help to remind management that the department lead going after your resources this year could have been you last year, but you didn't go after his or her resources. You'll only be accused of having missed an opportunity that might have prevented the precarious situation you find yourself in now. Better to have a strong story backed by numbers and go on the offensive by telling your story to everyone who matters.

## Find Your Story Stakeholders

The good thing about numbers is that you can prove *anything* with them. However, that's also a bad thing. Do you know this riddle? *If one person is in a room and two people walk out, another person must enter so the room becomes empty.* True or false? You can argue for either. This ridiculous statement demonstrates that numbers can show anything you want them to show. It's the persuasiveness of your number story that counts. Never forget that while you're telling your story, chances are someone else is telling an opposite story with the same numbers. Which story will the decision-makers buy?

To avoid competing with other storytellers when it really counts, always be on the offensive. Tell your story early and find others to share your story. Involve others so they feel invested. These people will become your story stakeholders. Early on, ask your manager for feedback to improve your story. When a manager helps shape a story, it's difficult not to defend it down the road. But one story stakeholder is not enough. To ensure your story is embraced by many stakeholders, it is best to shop it to other significant influencers in the company. This doesn't have to be an explicit ask; it's enough to seek feedback and explain that you highly value their opinions. If you ask the right questions, you can build their ideas into your story or at least refer to them later.

The ideal outcome of this proactive storytelling is twofold: First, your manager is fully on board because he or she is invested in the story from the outset. Second, referencing the interactions with other stakeholders will strengthen your position, especially if you come under fire. The numbers support your brilliant story to ensure it *can be* accepted. But it's proactive stakeholder management that will decide whether it *will be accepted*. As we all know, the best meetings *are those when all stakeholders have been briefed beforehand and are fully on board before the boardroom doors even open. This means no surprises, and that's exactly what you want.*

Leading is about mastering both your soft skills and your hard skills. When the two come together in a balanced way, it's a recipe for growth and high achievement. Your soft skills will enable your team to envision planting the flag at the top of Mount Everest, while your hard skills will map out the journey to get there. It's all about preventing and removing roadblocks along the way.

# Behavior Can't Wait

We all know human behavior doesn't change overnight. We also know culture is the driving force behind business results. If a culture is struggling because of unproductive or unhealthy human behaviors, a change in those behaviors is the only way to create a culture capable of achieving the desired business outcomes. This means productive and healthy behaviors must be learned and adopted by everyone in the culture. Shifting the behaviors of an individual can be difficult—even when it's our own behavior. But when an entire team, department, or company must make this type of shift, the task is much more complex and time-consuming. As everyone strives to adopt new behaviors, they must also shed old, ingrained ones. This requires hard work, commitment, and discipline. Behavioral changes, in turn, shift the dynamics between individuals and throughout the entire group, which is also a big adjustment for everyone. Some will adjust quickly, while others will struggle or resist. To complicate things even further, all of these positive changes must show up in people's day-to-day business activities, which might even influence processes. Meaningful cultural change is not for the faint of heart. There will be good and bad days. It will require time and patience. You'll need to track successes and setbacks, communicate with clarity, and encourage people to keep trying when the going gets tough. Once you've made a commitment to replace toxic behaviors with healthy ones, you can't go back. That's a recipe for disaster. The old behaviors you're trying to replace must actually stop, or you will break a sacred trust with your people, and they'll be unwilling to follow you through a change process again. That's a death knell for leaders, so don't do it.

Let me share some examples of what these important shifts look like from my own career. In one of my management roles, I was brought in to lead a team that had a "Yes, *but* . . ." problem. If you've managed teams, you've probably come across this behavior. Here's what it looks like in meetings: someone comes up with an interesting new idea, and the moment the words leave this person's lips, everyone starts raising their hands to explain why it's a bad idea and won't work. You'll hear things like, "We tried this before, but . . ." or "Great idea, but someone else has already done this . . ." or "Very clever suggestion, but the timing is bad . . ." or "Maybe if we had the resources, but . . ." There's not a single person willing to explore the idea or offer a follow-up question. This team is stuck. They've let creative thinking die on the vine. They're too afraid, lazy, or married to the past to embrace any new ideas, much less a new future filled with possibility. Over time, this sort of culture can be lethal for a company.

By the end of my first group meeting with this particular team, I knew my top priority must be to help them say goodbye to their "Yes, *but* . . ." culture and hello to a "Yes, *and* . . ." culture. After explaining how their "Yes, *but* . . ." behavior was hurting them as individuals and a team—and explaining how a "Yes, *and* . . ." attitude would change everything for the better—I asked them to participate in an experiment. They all agreed, and from that moment forward, if any of us said, "Yes, *but* . . ." we had to put $5 into a team box. We decided that once the money reached $300, it would fund a team dinner. If you can believe it, within two seconds, the first person raised his hand and said, "Yes, but I don't carry cash." Everyone started laughing. He brought cash the next day and was the first one to put $5 in the fund. We never reached our $300 goal, though I did take the team out for dinner to celebrate their positive behavior shift. It only took a couple of weeks for everyone to drop "Yes, *but* . . ." and start saying, "Yes, *and* . . ." It was apparent from the start of the experiment that people didn't want to be embarrassed for saying something they now understood was hindering their individual and group success. This negative behavior was quickly eradicated. Of course, the ingrained attitudes that fed the "Yes, *but* . . ." behavior lingered and required much more time and work, but a leader has to start somewhere—and words do matter. It might have been a small triumph, but it was a triumph nonetheless.

In another leadership role, I was asked to head a group of individuals who were self-promoters with little sense of what it meant to work as a team. They had a can-do spirit but lacked a we're-in-this-together approach. Everyone was out for themselves. In meetings with this team, people said things like, "*I* did this . . ." and "*I* said this . . ." and "*I* delivered this . . ." and "*My* idea was great . . ." There was no sense of collaboration, support, or gratitude. This petty culture had been nurtured by an immature former manager with a top-down mindset who was obsessively competitive. Instead of teaching his team to work together to achieve great things, he'd taught everyone to try to outdo their colleagues. One boasted about his higher budget, another her superior plan, another about his next big promotion, and another about how her jokes were the funniest. It was never-ending and exhausting! What a waste of time and energy! As a result, many talented people had left for other jobs. I explained to my new team why these childish and toxic behaviors had to stop. I was frank about what was at stake if they persisted with their competitive behaviors. And, once again, I challenged them to my $5 experiment. We agreed to immediately stop using sentences with the words *I*, *my*, *me*, or *mine* and start using ones that included *we* and *our*. Once they were aware of the problem, this can-do team made a remarkable and rapid shift. There was much more work needed to bring this team together, but changing this one behavior set the tone for more positive changes to come. People's words and behaviors matter! Behavior can't wait, so nip bad behavior in the bud when you see it, even if it means that results have to wait instead. This should be your top priority, especially with a new or inherited team.

## Make Yourself Dispensable

Yes, you read that correctly. The last step you must take after building, nurturing, and leading your high-performance team is to make sure you're not needed anymore. It's time for you to move on to new and potentially bigger things. If you have achieved your team-building goals and built a cohesive unit where everyone feels valued, contributes, and performs optimally both as individuals and as team players, you have done your job. Everyone is now working with a higher purpose in mind and is constantly crushing results and overshooting targets. Your team firmly believes the sky is the limit— or maybe that's shooting to low! They think and act big.

When you reach this point, you'll naturally feel proud of your team and yourself. But you could also feel something else, a feeling you might not like at first—you might not feel needed anymore. You might feel dispensable. This feeling can hit at any time, in a variety of situations. Maybe the budget plan was ironed out without your input. Perhaps an important contract with external partners had to be rewritten and this was done without you having to request the necessary changes. It could be that your team solved a vexing problem without you. These are all great developments, but they also signal that you are no longer needed the way you once were at the beginning of the team-building process. Trust me, this is a good thing—even if it stings a bit at first.

These signs that you're no longer needed will emerge slowly and steadily, not all at once. As they arise, it's time to remember your own career aspirations. What is your next important role? What is your next big endeavor? My advice is to move on with a strong foundation. Consider these three steps:

1.  Identify one or two individuals—from within or outside your organization—who can carry the torch and build upon what you have started. Begin grooming both as your potential successors. Two is better than one, because this gives you a choice as to which person ultimately will be the best fit to replace you when you are ready to leave.

2.  Include major stakeholders in the grooming and decision-making process about your successor. If you keep these stakeholders fully in the loop, they are more likely

to support your final choice. Always remember that once you move on, others must live with your successor choice. Choose wisely and with them in mind.

3.   Capitalize on your unique selling proposition. As you consider new roles, other people will be considering whether you can replicate your success in a different position or perhaps with a larger group. You need to start letting the world know you are definitely up for the challenge. These are the moments in your career when greater responsibility and upward mobility are possible. Through your team-building success, you've created a valuable currency you can use to promote yourself. You're sitting on a pot of gold. Use it to your advantage. It won't hold its value forever, so don't squander it.

Never minimize what you've achieved as a successful leader. Not only have you generated opportunities for yourself, you have also created opportunities for your team and your successor. Your team keeps thriving because your replacement lives and breathes what you have helped build. In fact, your entire team believes in your methods because you have proven—through their success—that these methods work. There's a lot of positive energy in these moments, so enjoy it!

# Section II

# On Strategy

Strategy without tactics is the slowest route to victory. Tactics without strategy is the noise before defeat.

—Sun Tzu, *The Art of War* [54]

# Overview

Ask five different people to define strategy and you'll get ten different definitions. Why ten? Because no one can articulate it in one go. Even if they can't quite define the term, everyone is still *doing* strategy. At most companies, there's an annual strategy plan, a long-term strategic plan, a three- or five-year strategy, and so on. Yet, no two business leaders agree on what's required to create a winning strategy. For some, it consists of three steps. For others, it's four pillars, or five components, or six elements. I'm not interested in adding another oversophisticated idea to this mix. In this book, we're not going to talk about understanding the customer, market, value drivers, or competition—or even how to navigate your cost base to achieve your P&L targets. For this knowledge, we went to business school. Instead, we're going to a different level, one people usually don't talk about, to get our bearings and talk about the *real* reasons why strategies sometimes work and sometimes don't. Let me share what I have learned by doing strategy for more than thirty years:

- Strategy is about having a plan to go most effectively and efficiently from A to a well-defined B and executing on that plan. But B must always ensure the company stays alive and prospers across changing markets and times.

- Strategy must lead to growth. If a company doesn't grow, it dies. And by growth, I mean financial growth. Therefore, strategy is always financial—no matter what.

- Strategy is worthless if it cannot be implemented. In the immortal words of Sun Tzu, in his book *The Art of War*, "Strategy without tactics is the slowest route to victory. Tactics without strategy is the noise before defeat."

- Structure follows strategy, not the other way around. Only adequate structure guarantees successful implementation.

- Finally, a company's culture must be actively managed in parallel with its strategy while traveling through markets and times. If you can't juggle both effectively while still moving your company forward, your culture will eat you, your strategy, and your company alive.

While these ideas may seem simple and straightforward, their implementation is not. Companies of all sizes, even successful ones, struggle to build and implement effective, sustainable strategies. Why? Because leaders don't lead businesses; they lead the people who do the business. Yes, you're going to hear this phrase throughout this book. It's people who create the strategy, lead its implementation, and execute its various tactics. At every level of every organization, people are the key to success or failure. And people, as we learned in section I, don't always understand people.

In a September 2020 McKinsey article titled "The Boss Factor: Making the World a Better Place through Workplace Relationships," authors Tera Allas and Bill Schaninger wrote: "When it comes to employee happiness, bosses and supervisors play a bigger role than one might guess. Relationships with management are the top factor in employees' job satisfaction, which in turn is the second most important determinant of employees' overall well-being . . . Unfortunately, research also shows that most people find their managers to be far from ideal; for example, in a recent survey, 75 percent of survey participants said that the most stressful aspect of their job was their immediate boss."[55] The global COVID-19 pandemic only magnified these problems. None of this points to an optimal environment for the creation and implementation of successful strategies. But what can be done?

Anytime people are working with people, there are opportunities and perils. Those who understand what drives human behavior have a distinct advantage when it comes to maximizing opportunities and minimizing perils. That's why the first section of this leadership book was "On People" and provided insights to help leaders build and lead successful teams. We learned how the right people and their behaviors in their respective environments are foundational to business success. We learned about how brains of *Homo sapiens* have evolved over hundreds of thousands of years, which means that in any human environment, there are always evolutionary traps, such as our predisposition for fear and anxiety in stressful situations because they are powerful survival strategies.

One of humanity's other highly successful survival strategies is not to change things for change's sake. Why would you? In our earliest days as humans, if you were able to put enough food on the table for everyone in your family to eat, your chances for survival were greatly improved. Why would you mess with such a good thing? Even if someone told you to leave your fertile, green valley with abundant animals and crops because there might be a flood in a year or two, you probably wouldn't leave. Maybe that's the evolutionary explanation for Noah only being able to get his family to leave with him on the arc—and all those animals, of course. Think about it, why would you jeopardize everything you've built just because there *might* be a flood someday? The risk-benefit ratio was just different back then. Our instincts—shaped by evolution—told us *not* to do new things, *not* to take risks, *not* to change. As modern humans, we're still wired to avoid change unless absolutely necessary.

But as we know, this approach does not work so well in today's fast-paced business climate. It is every business leader's biggest roadblock when it comes to strategy, which requires continuous change. The best book written about our reluctance to change, in my opinion, is *Who Moved My Cheese* by Dr. Spencer Johnson.[56] I had all my kids read this classic business and life parable. If you haven't read this book, I highly recommend it. At a minimum, it will help you confront your own evolutionary aversion to change, which is important if you have any role in shaping or executing strategy.

In addition to convoluted definitions and evolutionary biases, there's another challenge around strategy: leadership. Why do we even need leadership around strategy? Can't we just agree to move together as a group? This is easier said than done. As discussed in section I, we are more successful as individuals and as a species when we collaborate. Groups make it easier for us to bring down a giant mammoth, so working together increases our chances of survival. However, if a group simply rushes to kill a mammoth without a plan, the collaboration is likely to be much less effective than if activities are coordinated. That's why the best mammoth hunters were made leaders. They had a plan to move the group in the same direction to effectively accomplish an important goal. If the concept of leadership had not been beneficial, it would not have evolved as a human behavior. Of course, wherever there is leadership, there must be followership, a topic that is far too seldom discussed. Leaders don't exist without followers. In our early days as humans, followership also held benefits for both the individual and the group, and thus evolved as another important human behavior.

So, we know that evolution makes change hard for people. We also know leadership and followership have benefits for individuals and groups. This begs the question: What type of leader is capable of getting a reluctant group of humans to embrace change together in a coordinated fashion in pursuit of a common goal? It's a loaded question, and there is not just one answer.

In their academic research paper, "The Evolutionary Psychology of Leadership: Theory, Review, and Roadmap," published in the *Organizational Psychology Review*, authors Mark van Vugt and Richard Ronay found "three major barriers for effective leadership in organizations, (a) mismatches between modern and ancestral environments, (b) leader decision-making biases, and (c) evolved psychological mechanisms for dominance."[57] And this is where the answer to our question gets interesting.

## From Task Leadership to Corporate Graveyard

In humankind's earliest days, leadership was straightforward: the strongest person became the leader. As humankind survived, thrived, and cocreated, group dynamics became more complex. There were more groups, more people in each group, and groups in charge of other groups. Humans began to specialize and were asked to lead when their unique skills were required. If houses or ships needed to be built, those who knew how to build them took the lead. The same was true for agriculture, war, and most other activities. Those with the required skills led the way. It was wise to follow the warlord into war and let him choose the weapons. It was smart to let the ship-builder select the best trees to use to build the boats. The farmer with the most successful crops was naturally the go-to person during planting season. When these skilled individuals told us what to do, we followed their recommendations. Extrapolating from anthropo-logical evidence of past and present hunter-gatherer societies, we have a good understanding of this type of task-related leadership. It's a bottom-up approach that fosters universally positive leadership characteristics like integrity, persistence, humility, competence, deci-siveness, and vision, according to Vugt and Ronay's research. In such an environment, it was easy to check a leader's performance because success or failure was straightforward. People were promoted based on their mastery of a specific skill. If a ship sank once put to water, the shipbuilder was out. If the crops failed, the farmer was replaced. If the warlord lost, he didn't lead the next battle. Simple, right?

Compare this to today's leadership selection process in corporations. A person gets selected by a few senior leaders because they want him or her in a particular position for a specific assignment for a few years. Research suggests the traits that might have landed this person the job—overconfidence or an inflated sense of self—actually set this person up for failure when they find themselves completely out of their depth. The traits and skills that got them the promotion don't translate into effective leadership—and yet we still follow them. Why? Because our brains tell us this leader has led something successfully in the past so they will be able to lead us successfully again—even though their new role is completely different. No one thinks about the reality that some have even gotten the position because they are not good enough. Who would benefit from that? Well, what about the leader who put the person there in order to not get challenged and to get things through without resistance? Sound familiar? But even when this person sets the wrong strategy, we still follow them. We don't speak up. If some dare to, chances are others will tell them to shut up because this leader knows better, has the right network, and so forth. Our evolutionary bias toward followership compels us to keep following even bad leaders. Corporate graveyards are littered with ill-equipped leaders who decided on the wrong strategy and killed their business. Our evolutionary biases play a big role in every aspect of this destructive cycle.

## Evolutionary Mismatches

Our evolution is at the heart of many modern business problems. Remember that last survey you filled out and how it *surprisingly* identified a company- or department-wide communication issue? It's because, as Vugt and Ronay referenced in their research, "the environment that most of us live in is very different from the environment that our ancestors lived in only some 13,000 years ago, before the advent of agriculture. From 2.5 million years ago—when the first hominids appeared in Africa—until the agricultural revolution, humans lived in relatively small nomadic band societies of around 150 individuals at maximum, leading a hunter-gatherer lifestyle. Further, fossil evidence indicates that human brain size has remained remarkably stable for at least the last 200,000 years. This leads some evolutionary psychologists to conclude that 'our modern skulls house a Stone Age mind' (Tooby & Cosmides, 1997) with the potential for significant mismatches."[58] It wasn't until the Industrial Revolution in the mid-eighteenth century that we started working together in large corporations. And look at us now. In an evolutionary blink of an eye, we have gigantic national and multinational corporations with hundreds, thousands, or even tens of thousands of employees spread across the globe. Add to this the rapid social media evolution where a message can be distributed, read, and interpreted (or misinterpreted, or even shared with the intent to be misinterpreted) by millions of people in seconds. Of course we have communication issues! Our evolution hasn't prepared us for this type of work environment. The growth has happened and continues to happen way too quickly for evolutionary adaptation to keep up.

Evolution has prepared us to work successfully in small groups. Yet, as leaders, we're now asked to achieve strategic alignment in companies with tens of thousands of employees. Walmart, one of the biggest employers in the world, has around 2.1 million employees![59] No, that's not a typo. The strategic leadership challenges there must be daunting. There's a reason we talk about a reasonable "span of control" when it comes to leadership positions. You can lead five people, or maybe even ten, for a short period of time, but you can't directly lead twenty or hundreds or thousands. When we try to expand our span of control to unreasonable levels, it results in very tangible strategy and communication disconnects. Employees end up heads down, working in little silos, unaware of the company's latest strategies. If you don't believe me, pick up the phone and call a few of your fellow department leads. Ask them what the three most important imperatives or critical success factors are for your company's strategy this year. I guarantee no one will give you the same answer.

In a *Harvard Business Review* article titled "The Office of Strategy Management," Robert S. Kaplan and David P. Norton wrote: "Our research reveals that, on average, 95 percent of a company's employees are unaware of, or do not understand, its strategy. If the employees who are closest to customers and who operate processes that create value are unaware of the strategy, they surely cannot help the organization implement it effectively."[60] Between what we know about the evolution of the human brain and a growing body of studies about modern leadership challenges, the evidence is clear: it's nearly impossible to build awareness and attain alignment across very large groups. Unfortunately, this reality hasn't stopped us from throwing unprepared leaders into untenable situations.

Instead of taking a hard look at the way leaders are selected, promoted, and prepared, companies still obsess about fixing their communication problems. It's easier to address a couple of symptoms instead of tackling the real, underlying problems. Those of you who have been involved in such fixes know they never work—never. But this doesn't keep the same ridiculous cycle from occurring over and over. Tackling humanity's evolutionary wiring and today's tough cultural and organizational challenges just seems too daunting. The "mismatches between modern and ancestral environments" that Vugt and Ronay identified are very real and problematic. It's time for modern leaders to understand and address them—to take on the mammoth in the room.

Vugt and Ronay's second barrier to effective strategic leadership addresses underlying decision-making biases. They have cited a large body of research documenting how decision-making biases impact human judgment and reveal themselves in "traits that might emerge from overconfidence, such as lack of self-awareness, inflated self-evaluations, defensiveness in the face of error, and failure to learn from experience."[61] We've all seen and experienced these behaviors in the workplace. These traits—which never lead to constructive problem-solving or effective decision-making—combined with the cognitive biases explored by evolutionary psychologists through the lens of error-management theory lead to businesses being either overly conservative or outrageously risky in precisely the wrong moments.[62] [63] Finding the right balance and navigating these evolutionary biases can be more art than science. However, this must be mastered—and science can help. The impacts these biases have on decision-making are too profound to ignore. We'll explore this more later in this section.

Vugt and Ronay's third barrier for effective leadership in organizations, evolved psychological mechanisms for dominance, compliments the second barrier: "Humans have evolved psychological mechanisms designed to dominate and exploit others, ascend social hierarchies, and prevent rivals from achieving dominance . . . Dominance is still part of our ancient primate heritage and there is plenty of evidence from traditional and modern societies that leaders will coerce followers if they believe they can get away with it."[64] [65] While no one likes this, we have to acknowledge that this behavior is part of our evolutionary makeup. This means expressing dominance can have benefits for a person's individual fitness, even if it has negative implications for others. One need look no further than politics, be it local or global, to see examples. War, terror, crime, and so forth are just some of the negative results the world experiences when powerful individuals use their status to consolidate power, enrich themselves, and dominate. The negative results might be different in an office setting, but they are still destructive, especially for those trying to create successful, sustainable strategies. Still, these barriers show up in the workplace every day because they are not addressed or managed. Over time, they can have a huge negative impact on a company's strategy. It doesn't have to be this way. What is best for the entire *company* should guide the strategy—not someone's need for dominance. If all the power rests in the hands of one or a few leaders, and there are not the appropriate frameworks available to keep that power in check, everyone kowtows, because leaders control salaries, promotions, and so much more. Over time, people's feelings of helplessness impact innovation, strategy, and problem-solving. Leaders need to constantly remind themselves of their evolutionary tendency to dominate. Attitudes and behaviors need to be checked accordingly.

It's time to focus on the *real* reasons strategies go wrong. It's not because your market research department does not know how to secure accurate competitor insights or because the manufacturing department has no clue how to properly calculate the output of a production line. Strategies are derailed because leaders don't understand or even consider the powerful impact of their own evolutionary biases and those of their people. Nor do they understand the social dynamics of people trying to work in big groups and dealing with continuous change, both of which are often incompatible with our evolutionary beliefs about safety, as well as leadership and followership. Announcing a strategy out of the blue and expecting everyone to jump on board and toe the line is a pipe dream that ignores thousands of years of human evolution. As I've mentioned several times—because it's very important—your organization's culture must be actively managed in parallel with your strategy while continuing to move forward through ever-changing markets and times. It's an epic undertaking. But until this happens, your strategies will continue to fail. As you know all too well, the stakes are often high when it comes to strategy. Human behavior either clarifies and strengthens a company's strategic vision or blurs it until it's unrecognizable. Which would you prefer? Let's dig into these topics further so we can significantly increase your chances of developing successful and sustainable strategies.

# Chapter 5

# Recognize Tomorrow's Company Is Today's Everyday Business

I am from Austria. It is a beautiful country that attracts many visitors every year, especially skiers and hikers during the winter and spring months. Amateur mountain hikers and once-a-year skiers flock to the world-famous Alps by the thousands. It's great for the Austrian economy, but not so great for the mountain guides and alpine rescue units. You see, every year, a good number of tourists overestimate their physical abilities and underestimate the Alps. Either they don't pay attention or choose to willfully ignore the many weather and avalanche warnings—even though these warnings are *everywhere*. These tourists look at the beautiful morning sky above, blue as a robin's egg, and assume everything will be fine for the rest of the day. They optimistically set off into the mountains with their fancy gear, maybe some food, and fashionable, light clothing. A few hours later, bad weather moves in suddenly and a few tourists go missing in the storm, end up trapped by an avalanche, or sometimes both. Rescue missions are formed. Helicopters, mountaineers, alpine rescue divisions with rescue dogs, and emergency medical staff are called out into unsafe conditions to search for the lost tourists—often risking their lives to save others. Luckily, due to hundreds of years of traditional mountaineering knowledge and expert modern training, most of the missing tourists are found and rescued. The injured are flown down the mountains by highly trained helicopter pilots who defy wind gusts and the laws of physics to bring the victims to specialized mountain hospitals or university clinics with trained trauma units, doctors, and nurses. Somehow, these skilled professionals are usually able to patch up all the broken bones, torn tissues, and crushed organs.

Most of these injured tourists regret their mistake and learn a life-altering lesson. But there are always a few who think they were just unlucky, that they encountered some sort of weather anomaly or rented faulty equipment. Even when they disagree about *how* they got themselves into such a dangerous situation, all of them agree on two points: First, the rescue teams—the searchers, mountaineers, pilots, and medical staff, even the dogs—did an amazing job. Second, they never want to find themselves in this type of situation again.

Every year, hundreds if not thousands of companies *suddenly* find themselves in *unforeseeable* circumstances despite plenty of warnings signs. The leadership team claims no one could have ever imagined such scenarios, even though employees, advisors, and industry experts loudly and frequently warned them about it. They achieved their financial plans and all of their other goals. While the horizon grew a bit grayer every year, with more competitors entering the market—some of them with remarkable innovative approaches—market share shifts were only very minor, so who cares? The sky is still blue, there may be a few dark clouds far away, but in general, today and tomorrow still look still very good, and after all, the future does not happen that fast anyway. Well, usually what happens is that this goes on for years, many years. But then, one year, the company's results are not so great. *Suddenly,* the company needs to do something more than make some adjustments or reduce prices temporarily. When the realities of this year hit, the team at headquarters decide to confront the cold hard truth about an *unforeseeable* crisis. First and foremost, the executive team will start communicating about how difficult things are. They'll say things like, "This year's environment is more dynamic and unpredictable than expected, so a 'quick change' is necessary." Then, leadership will call in the rescue team—you remember, the mountaineers, the alpine teams with their search dogs, and the emergency medical staff. Oops, wrong story! Let's try again. Leadership will call in a flurry of strategy and crisis consultants, change experts, lawyers, financial analysts, and statistical wizards with PhDs in mathematical physics to save what is left of a once-thriving company. All the data and insights will be gathered during the crisis and crunched into models, programs, and case studies to be presented in a series of highly facilitated "change workshops" where impressively written "change stories" will help everyone pull together to patch up all the disorientated managers, torn apart structures, and crushed belief systems. Of course, all the people who were laid off to ensure the P&L fit the regional guidance and represented the correct SG&A as percentage of revenue were not invited. More often than not—thanks to decades of experience addressing comparable business crises—the company will be salvaged and learn a life-altering lesson about the dangerous pitfalls of lagging data, overconfidence, misinformation, and outdated practices, services, products, or all of the above.

Who would have thought there were so many parallels between skiing, hiking, and business? But now you know. There is one big difference, though. Unlike the tourists who praised the alpine rescue teams, business stakeholders typically praise *themselves*. That's right, the managers who led the company into this precarious situation in the first place—and were subsequently tasked with the "revolution-ary" change workshops and process to reverse the crisis—believe *they* did an amazing job rescuing the company. *They* underwent the right analysis. *They* made the right strategic and structural decisions. *They* were able to keep the company's top talent and ensure only expendable employees were laid off. (*They* overlook the fact that most of the top talent saw the crisis coming and left well before it hit—but these are just small details, right?) As *they* celebrate *their* successes, plenty of people in the organization begin talking to one another about how these were the same people who failed to identify and prepare for the storm, despite ample warnings. They wonder why these people are patting themselves on the back and getting promoted instead of fired. Meanwhile, the quick "changes" implemented to "turn things around" keep coming. Everyone knows these are not the healthy, intentional, evenly paced changes the company needs to survive and thrive again. Confidence and trust in leadership are lost, and employees feel helpless and hopeless. The culture is in a shambles.

## Continuous and Consistent Is Better

When business leaders call for change, the implication is almost always speed. A quick change might come in the form of a new product, an updated processor, or a new structure. In reality, these quick remedies should have been in place a long time ago, but in the moment, they appear to "fix the problem." The truth is that quick fixes are part of the problem. At too many companies, reacting to crisis after crisis is the main or only way change happens. Without realizing it, *this is their strategy*. Obviously, this is not enough. To uncover and fix the real systemic, underlying problems, leaders must dig deeper. Why did the company overlook or ignore an imminent reality? Why did the company fail to execute on its core strategy?

If companies can't address the root causes of these never-ending crises, they will continue to struggle with strategic growth—and ultimately experience stagnation or decline.

Sustainable growth requires effective management of the company's current position and strategy in tandem with its ongoing evolution in the face of ever-changing markets and times. Let's look at two global giants to see what this looks like in the real world. Kodak, which developed the first digital camera technology, is a good example of a company that refused to face ever-changing markets and times. The company's decision not to innovate due to concerns that new technology would jeopardize its film business ended up putting a stranglehold on its growth. What had brought Kodak to the top of its game—having a market-dominating core competency—ultimately became a hinderance to its evolution. The leadership team found it too difficult to leave the comfort of their market dominance to embark into unknown territory. This scenario is not uncommon in the corporate world. Unfortunately, when reality final hits and leaders realize the company's core competency is no longer relevant to consumers, it's often too late. This was the case for Kodak.[66]

It's not easy for leaders to keep their foot on the day-to-day business while continually evolving in the face of ever-changing markets and times. But it is far superior to the alternative, which is constantly slamming on the breaks in a crisis and then thumping a foot on the accelerator with a quick, reactive "fix." This approach is inefficient, jarring, and burns up too much fuel too fast. Ultimately, it's not an effective way to drive growth (pun intended). One can only imagine the leadership discussions at Kodak between those who saw the coming demise of existing camera technology and those looking at their colorful pie charts that showed Kodak at the top of its market. When the writing was finally on the wall, the leaders who clung to the past had to acknowledge that their halfhearted attempt to catch up was too little too late. Sadly, the company faded away over the course of the next decade before filing for bankruptcy. It didn't have to end that way. The company certainly had the tech and talent to innovate, but their leaders did not have the courage to embrace the necessary change to support that innovation. The Kodak story demonstrates how tough it can be to effectively manage a company's current position and strategy in tandem with necessary, ongoing evolution in the face of ever-changing markets and times.

Nokia Mobile Phones (NMP) is another strong example of this destructive phenomenon. The company rapidly grew into one of the most recognizable brands in the world, at one point commanding more than 40 percent of global market share in mobile phones. But by 2013, Nokia was in decline, and its mobile phone business was sold to Microsoft. In his book, *Ringtone*, author Yves Doz, *professor emeritus of strategic management at INSEAD,* explores the strategic decisions that contributed to the epic rise and fall of Nokia.[67]

It is tempting to lay the blame for Nokia's demise at the doors of Apple, Google and Samsung. But . . . this ignores one very important fact: Nokia had begun to collapse from within well before any of these companies entered the mobile communications market. In these times of technological advancement, rapid market change and growing complexity, analyzing the story of Nokia provides salutary lessons for any company wanting to either forge or maintain a leading position in their industry . . .

NMP became locked into an increasingly conflicted product development matrix between product line executives with P&L responsibility and common "horizontal resource platforms" whose managers were struggling to allocate scarce resources. They had to meet the various and growing demands of increasingly numerous and disparate product development programs without sufficient software architecture development and software project management skills. This conflictual way of working slowed decision-making and seriously dented morale, while the wear and tear of extraordinary growth combined with an abrasive CEO personality also began to take their toll. Many managers left.

Beyond 2004, top management was no longer sufficiently technologically savvy or strategically integrative to set priorities and resolve conflicts arising in the new matrix. Increased cost reduction pressures rendered Nokia's strategy of product differentiation through market segmentation ineffective and resulted in a proliferation of poorer quality products . . .

While Nokia posted some of its best financial results in the late 2000s, the management team was struggling to find a response to a changing environment: Software was taking precedence over hardware as the critical competitive feature in the industry. At the same time, the importance of application ecosystems was becoming apparent, but as dominant industry leader Nokia lacked the skills, and inclination to engage with this new way of working.

It's striking how similar the two stories are, isn't it? Nokia and Kodak, both top brands, squandered their market-leading positions because they basically refused to adapt. It's a huge problem—and it's much more common than leaders care to admit. The reality is that it's extremely challenging to effectively manage a company's current position and strategy while also navigating ongoing evolution in the face of ever-changing markets and times. But it's not impossible.

## Organizational Change Theory

There are only two major classes of change processes: class one, which is vision induced, and class two, which is problem induced.[vi] With class one, change can be achieved through evolutionary development (gradual, continuous change over time) or through strategic revolutionary change (rapid transformation over a shorter period of time). Evolutionary development happens in organizations where the culture is actively managed to evolve alongside ongoing change. The process is gradual and perpetual—just like human evolution. On the other hand, strategic revolutionary change requires companies to prepare their cultures for big shifts as well. If a company has a solid business development pillar that states it will buy other companies to acquire new products or technologies, then that company's culture needs to be prepared to handle big changes before and after every acquisition. While riskier than evolutionary development, strategic revolutionary change can be successful with a strong plan in place to support the company's people and culture. Class one change processes are proactive and typically lead to positive outcomes.

Class two change processes are radical and reactive. They're the choice when things are not going according to plan or leadership is surprised by something they probably should have seen coming. This means one of the company's strategic pillars, maybe the entire business model, is in trouble. There's a rescue mission underway because something went wrong, was overlooked, or was ignored. Class two change processes are popular for crisis management because evolutionary development is not possible in these situations. There's no time, so the company always ends up in a revolutionary change process, but without the necessary preparation or strategy. The culture must be prepared to handle big changes in a short amount of time, which is far from ideal. For all the reasons we've already discussed, class two change processes are adopted way more often than class one change processes. It's unfortunate but true. I've seen this throughout my career: a crisis is covered, maybe in some cases averted, with class two change processes, but the cost is high and the return limited.

With only two major classes, change looks straightforward in theory. Leaders only need to be proactive, have a strong strategic plan, and prepare their cultures for either evolutionary development or strategic revolutionary change. And there's one more important element: this transformation needs to happen strategically and on a constant basis. Only then can a company experience evolutionary change. There is never a time when a company should not be transforming itself. Businesses are constantly on the move through markets and times. But because change from an evolutionary perspective will always feel uncomfortable, too many leaders neglect these realities and requirements. They fail to see the writing on the wall and embrace the necessary forward-thinking strategic planning. Of the few who seem to acknowledge the need for constant transformation, many of them relegate the most important of all factors—the human element—and relegate corporate culture to the sidelines. Then, when the latest crisis "sneaks up on them," they are ill-prepared. Unfortunately, this means class two change processes are their only choice. When this becomes the norm, it sets in motion a vicious cycle and things deteriorate.

## Evolution Is Everyday Business

To avoid the downward spiral of reactive class two change processes, companies must make a corporate-wide commitment to class one change processes. Existing as a formidable marketplace player in five, ten, or fifteen years is the strategic North Star for every company, and this can only be achieved through class one change processes, preferably evolutionary development.

So, how does a leadership team undertake this type of gradual, continuous change over time? Well, *not* by exclusively protecting current core competencies. That was Kodak's mistake. You might ask, "How can we know whether to let go or stay invested in our core competencies?" This isn't really the right question to ask. The better question is, "How can we manage the company's current positioning in unison with its continuous, incremental transformation?" *This* is an important question to ponder from a leadership perspective. Remember, in strategically forward-looking businesses, there is no such thing as quick, radical change. Change in these healthy businesses is continuous, mostly incremental, and always proactive.

There is also no such thing as "starting innovation." Either your company has built an utmost fearless culture that fosters innovation every day in every department and team (even if that means some necessary failures), or it has not. If you suddenly discover that your competitors have more innovative solutions than you, or that the marketplace environment has changed quickly, then, unfortunately, you do not have an innovative culture, and it might already be too late. Upon realizing this, it will not help to kick off a one-month "how to innovate" workshop series or any other reactionary initiative to calm your nerves. Trust me, I've seen these panicky responses fail many times in my career. A leader cannot go to bed on Monday, get up on Tuesday, and say, "Today is the day we're becoming innovative!" Continuous adaptation must be part of a company's culture, embraced and practiced by its people, and embedded in the organization's DNA. If people are afraid to discuss change or question the status quo because of arrogant or intolerant leadership, an outside consultant or workshop series isn't going to fix the issue. The change must start at the top and permeate throughout the entire company. This takes time, a clear plan, and a strong, ongoing commitment from an effective executive team.

Via his systemic model of corporate leadership, economics professor and lecturer Dr. Peter Herbek explains how *everything* companies do today must be continuously vetted through the lens of time.[vi] Herbek believes that whenever you think of strategy, structure, or culture, you must also consider how each of these ensures that the current business goals align with the company's continuous transition into the future. These concepts need to be consciously adopted. If not, the company will always fall victim to current operational problems and will fail to evolve. But, let's be honest, who among us is constantly asking, "How do my current strategies and structures evolve with our company over the next two, five, or ten years?" We're all too busy juggling all our daily responsibilities to think about this, much less answer that question. And, of course, it's not even worth pondering this question if nobody knows what the company should look like or what its position in the marketplace should be in two, five, or ten years. If the goal is to keep the company dynamically stable on its journey through markets and times, it's important to know where the organization is headed. To paraphrase Einstein's famous quotes, business is like riding a bicycle—to keep your balance, you must keep moving. But if you don't know where you're going, what's the point? Time to install a GPS on your bicycle.

Herbek's model of corporate leadership is clever and highly useful. It shows all the important areas to manage in parallel with conscious transformation management. It's a great foundation, but I believe there is more to it. A specific order must be recognized for these activities to happen successfully in the real world as part of the daily grind. Certain activities should take priority over others. Additionally, achieving dynamic stability while evolving through markets and times rarely means you're working on one thing. What makes this process so powerful, when correctly implemented, is that the future-building activities are constantly vetted against day-to-day business priorities and vice versa. This ensures that all business elements are continuously adjusted toward one another. Together, they play into the company's long-term vision, including the results, culture, and positioning for the future. Because this is a dynamic, multilayered activity, a feedback mechanism is also vital.

## Change Is More Than Innovation

When leaders think of the future, often only innovation immediately comes to mind. But this view is incomplete. The basics of the business must change alongside innovation. Remember, innovation is not a goal, it's an intentional mindset that top-performing companies embrace. Even if an organization has an effective, efficient, sustainable business model, constant adaptation and innovation are required to keep everything aligned with the company's vision for the future—that's right, riding a bicycle with a GPS. If the leadership team isn't clear on the business's basics today, and their current impact on customers and competition, then things are being done in the wrong order. Do you know how impactful your current product positioning and messaging is? Do you have well-defined strategies in place? Are you sure your sales force is executing successfully based on this strategy? What about your distribution system—is it efficient and reliable? Whatever the basics are for your business and your industry, those must be in good working order before you can start thinking about an evolution model. Address the issues that provide stability and pay the rent today and you'll create a strong foundation that allows for dynamically evolving future strategies.

## Consider Decision Science

Human decision-making has evolved significantly throughout human evolution. Early humans relied on simple instincts and immediate sensory feedback to make decisions that were critical for their survival, such as whether to fight or flee in the face of a threat or where to find food and water. These decisions were often rooted in basic heuristics and relied on limited cognitive resources.

As human societies became more complex, decision-making evolved to encompass cooperation and collaboration. Group dynamics became crucial for survival and reproduction. This led to the development of more advanced decision-making processes, including the ability to assess the trustworthiness of others and make decisions about with whom to form alliances. In today's complex social environment, human decision-making is influenced by a wide range of cognitive biases, which can sometimes lead to suboptimal choices. Some of the most notable biases include:

- Confirmation Bias: People tend to seek out and give more weight to information that confirms their existing beliefs and ignore contradictory information.

- Availability Heuristic: Individuals tend to overestimate the importance of information readily available to them.

- Anchoring and Adjustment: People tend to anchor their decisions based on the first piece of information they encounter and then make adjustments from there.

- Status Quo Bias: Individuals prefer the status quo and are resistant to change, even when it may be in their best interest.

- Groupthink: Individuals often adopt the majority opinion to maintain harmony and avoid conflict, even if it leads to suboptimal decisions.

- Loss Aversion: People tend to place a higher value on avoiding losses than on acquiring equivalent gains.

- Recency Bias: Recent events are often given more weight in decision-making.

- Self-Serving Bias: People tend to attribute positive outcomes to their abilities and negative outcomes to external factors, enhancing their self-esteem.

- Other biases include hindsight bias, illusion of control, escalating commitment, etc.

These and other biases influence various aspects of our lives, including our business and leadership decisions. Recognizing these biases is essential if we want to improve the quality of our decision-making. While critical thinking and self-awareness can help to mitigate the impact of these biases, when it comes to business decisions, it is highly recommended to support your ultimate decision-making process through decision science, which, in my experience, is still a highly underrated and underused discipline.

This interdisciplinary field combines elements of mathematics, statistics, psychology, and other disciplines to help businesses make informed and optimal decisions. It leverages data-driven approaches and analytical techniques to guide the decision-making process. Here are just some of the characteristics, processes, and tools that guide decision science:

- Quantitative Analysis: Mathematical models, statistical methods, and algorithms help quantify uncertainties, risks, and the benefits associated with various options. As opposed to human biases, this leads to an understanding of past trends and outcomes, allowing businesses to make decisions based on empirical evidence rather than gut feelings or intuition.

- Predictive Analytics: Forecasting future scenarios and outcomes by analyzing historical data informs predictions so leaders can make proactive decisions.

- Scenario Analysis: Assessing multiple scenarios and their respective outcomes allows organizations to prepare for various contingencies and select the best course of action.

- Decision Support Systems: Called DSS for short, these computer-based tools can assist in decision-making by providing real-time data, analytics, and visualizations.

- Risk Management: Decision science provides businesses with tools to evaluate and manage risks associated with decisions. This includes risk assessment, risk mitigation strategies, and the development of risk management frameworks.

- Cost-Benefit Analysis: This type of analysis helps to quantify costs versus benefits in various scenarios, ensuring businesses make choices that offer the most favorable return on investment.

These are just examples, and if you want to know more about it, I suggest you look up Martin Peterson's book *An Introduction to Decision Theory*.[68] In summary, decision science equips businesses with tools, methodologies, and processes to make more informed, rational, and data-driven decisions. It provides the opportunity to put all options on the table and make fewer bias-driven decisions.

## The Most Important Thing

"The most important thing is to keep the most important thing the most important thing." I first heard this phrase in 2005, when a colleague quoted it as we were discussing how he was leading his company through a major change process. I was amused by the saying's conversational tone and simplicity. It made perfect sense. Over the years, I have used this phrase to remind myself about the need to prioritize. In fact, this sentence is probably the single most important piece of professional advice I have ever received. If you apply the wisdom of this phrase - in either your professional or personal life - you become fearless and unstoppable. You know exactly what you need to do.

When my friend said this to me back in 2005, I loved my job but was juggling a complex mix of strategic and practical business and cultural challenges. My days were filled with unknowns. I was also working through several career firsts but didn't yet have a network of colleagues to advise and guide me. As you can imagine, I felt overwhelmed. While the goals I was supposed to achieve were clearly defined, everything on the path to achieving them seemed complex and confusing. Where should I begin? What was the best order in which to tackle competing interests?

I applied the most-important-thing logic to the situation. I had a huge wall in my office, so I filled it with *every* business dependency that influenced the strategic and tactical decision-making process. I was astonished by the interconnectedness of everything. How was I going to digest all this, make sense of it, and explain it to others? Then, something clicked: if I could step away from the strategic pillars, break things down, allow myself to think beyond strategy, and decipher the details even all the way down to potential tactical implications and likelihoods rather than just desired outcomes, I would finally be able to see the forest for the trees.

Nobel Prize for Peace winner Desmond Tutu, said it well: *"There is only one way to eat an elephant: a bite at a time."* All too often, leaders shy away from the hard work of thinking about strategy with implementation in mind. But believe me, only then is one able to put the right priorities, interdependencies, and orders to any business situation. You have to identify the most important thing—the first bite—to see the next one and the next one. This also helps you decide what not to do, which is equally important. Since I'm quoting smart people, I'll throw in Michael Porter's famous saying, *"The essence of strategy is choosing what not to do."*[69] So true!

I don't want to imply that identifying the single most important thing in any situation is a completely binary process. That would be oversimplifying—and misleading. As professionals, we are constantly multitasking, running many different projects at the same time. Typically, pressure mounts from all sides, and it feels like everything needs to happen all at once. But when your decisions have an impact on many different projects, isn't it even more important to make the most important thing the most important thing? The art of this process is to learn how to listen past the chatter and distinguish relevant information from the noise, the critical from the clutter. Once you have done that, you know what's worth including in your thinking about the most important thing. It takes time to master this skill, but understanding and practicing it prepares you to think about strategy much more effectively.

## Structure Follows Strategy—Always

This concept seems so simple, yet we constantly get it wrong. Our brains immediately want to contemplate *how* we are going to do something, not *why* it's important or *what* it's going to accomplish. We think project plan and budget before objective. We think structure before strategy. That's backward.

If you start with structure, it's difficult to detach yourself from current considerations of what is possible. You are likely to fall victim to thoughts like, "Within the current environment, I can do this but not that . . ." This type of limited thinking immediately sets you up for failure. You end up doing more of what you've always done. Innovation can't happen if that's your mindset. Yes, you need to think about strategy with implementation in mind, but there's no contradiction, because they are two different things. The first one, strategy, is about what you need to do. The second one, implementation, is about *how* you do it once you have decided on the best strategic option.

Companies thinking within current, known, or approved structures while trying to find the best strategic approach to a problem can't reach their potential. In my opinion, this is one of the biggest reasons so many companies fall victim to reactionary and mediocre change processes when they face marketplace challenges and threats. One of my university business professors once said, "Organizations are only adapting to the extent they do not have to change" That's a powerful, discouraging, and illuminating statement. As we've discussed, from an evolutionary perspective, change is difficult for humans. Evolution has wired us to be wary of, well, evolution. But transformation is necessary and should be constant in business. If organisms do not constantly adapt and evolve, they die. If companies do not constantly adapt and evolve, they also die. What we know feels safe and comfortable, especially if it has been successful. It's difficult to leave that behind and navigate uncharted territories. But in business, what feels good today can become cumbersome and even dangerous tomorrow. This is why we must always go back to riding our GPS-enabled bicycle. And what's the most important thing to know when riding a GPS-enabled bicycle? After you check the tires are aired and the gears well-oiled, the most important thing to know is where you're going and how to make the bike move forward in that direction. Structure follows strategy. The goal is to keep your bike dynamically stable on its journey through markets and times and en route to your desired destination. Remember, if your strategy is to get to the top of a tall mountain and your current bike only has three gears, you might need to upgrade your bike. In the next chapter, I'll introduce a framework that can help.

# Chapter 6

# Apply a Dynamic Stability Business Framework

I created the Dynamic Stability Business Framework not because it introduces fundamentally new things that you've never heard of. In fact, you learned (or should have learned) about all of this in business school. The thing I did do, though, was put a simple system around it and call it a sequence of events to help you know how to think about it. Businesses, as I have mentioned, are not static entities. Rather, they are continuously evolving human systems that require adaptation and stability in equal parts. Even as leaders help their companies adapt to ever-changing markets and times, they must constantly vet today's actions in light of where the company is headed. And future plans must be vetted in light of current business priorities. This framework is strategic but designed with implementation in mind. Therefore, I've included applicable tactics to support the strategic intent. Strategy without implementation in mind is a theoretical exercise that helps no one. Remember Sun Tzu's saying that it's "the slowest way to victory." As a leader, your mission is to get the dynamics of continuous change aligned with the stability your current business needs to remain viable. But as we've already discussed, change is hard for organizations and the humans who do the work in those organizations. Evolutionary biases and day-to-day business get in the way. I have seen this over and over and over again throughout my career. To be sustainable, companies must build proactive cultures of continuous, incremental transformation.

## Create "Team Transformation"

If you dive directly into strategy without actively engaging, educating, and preparing your team, you're not setting yourself or your team up for success. Without a culture fit, there's no foundation for the future; things are likely to fall apart quickly. There are many reasons why change almost always feels uncomfortable. On the one hand, when things are running brilliantly, many will ask, "Why fix what's not broken?" That's our evolutionary bias against change speaking, as we've already discussed. On the other hand, when things are running poorly, people understand that change is needed—but potentially, that realization has come too late. Both scenarios are a challenge. The long-term goal is to integrate transformation into everyday business, to make openness to continuous transformation and evolution part of the culture's DNA. This means changing a lot of hearts and minds, which begins with baby steps.

First, your team must understand and support the new framework and be prepared for the changes its implementation will bring. Address the elephant—or better yet, the mammoth—in the room: those evolutionary biases that will kick into high gear and make people feel unsure, uncomfortable, and hesitant about upcoming changes. To help people overcome these powerful biases, build a team of change champions around you. Call them "Team Evolution" or some other aspirational term aligned with your strategic intent. This team must be built very intentionally. The right people are key. Do not invite only senior members to join this team. Gather a good mix of innovative, creative, and visionary employees from different levels in the company. These should be people who don't take the status quo for granted and are, in general, quite fearless by nature. You need this mix of people from different corporate levels and departments to facilitate wide acceptance of the framework and help it gain traction. Make sure one person on the team knows something about group moderation and innovation. Find a senior sponsor, like a general manager. But make sure it's the type of person who is prepared to get his or her hands dirty with the team. Avoid a strawman sponsor who hangs around on paper but does not care. Agree on a cadence for this new team to meet, collaborate, present their progress, and so forth. Give this team license to expand to the wider corporation. You don't want to overmanage the team or constrict their visionary thinking. Let them brainstorm and get creative with ideas like company-wide innovation competitions, forums, or writing competitions about the company's vision. These are just a few ideas, but you get my point. These change champions need corporate-wide visibility. Ensure proper continuous succession as people move on. Last but not least, incentivize team members with something other than money. You don't want to attract people who are only interested in the extra compensation. Find creative ways to compensate them for the additional tasks they are undertaking. You want to attract people who are passionate about the future. For example, you could invite them to a speaker series where team members could meet renowned innovation leaders. Maybe you have a special monthly dinner for them with a well-known person. There are so many ways to build an environment in which these special team members can find motivation and thrive. Of course, all of this does not count out monetary compensation for extra work done.

Once this team is in place, prepare them to develop the company's strategic vision and its pathway into the future. Give them time and license to look into all the possibilities. As their vision unfolds and takes shape, they will be able to help others throughout the organization see this vision. They will also show people how the framework can help everyone prepare for this new future and embrace change as part of their everyday work. They rally everyone around a vision for the next five, ten, and fifteen years, and the framework that can get them there.

If done well, such efforts can transform cultures and companies. One recent example of this type of transformative change comes from Jeep. The change agents in this company have imagined a future in which 50 percent of sales in the US and 100 percent of sales in Europe will be battery-electric vehicles (BEV) by 2030.[70] Imagine the hundreds of fascinating conversations that took place in this organization to bring about this bold and transformative commitment. It's a paradigm shift of epic proportions—and a great example of actively preparing for evolutionary change with a transformative, strategic vision in mind.

## Build a Proactive Culture of Transformation

To support the Dynamic Stability Business Framework and deal with change effectively—in a continuous, proactive fashion rather than a crisis-oriented, reactive fashion—a strong, evolved culture is required. As I've mentioned several times, this doesn't happen overnight. But I don't believe business strategies fail because people don't know *how* to do strategy; I believe they fail because people can't embrace the cultural transformation necessary to *support* new strategies. Proactively managed cultural transformation is the most important strategy of all. It is the key to success and growth. Waking up one morning and commanding everyone to embrace the future is not an acceptable framework for change—and it's absolutely doomed from the start. Instead, a series of incremental, intentional activities must be undertaken to support a new, change-oriented mindset that can shift the culture over time and help it become remarkable. Here are some tips:

- Create a very clear vision at the executive level, stating that proactive, incremental transformation is the most important strategy.

- Educate and train your people about humanity's evolutionary biases against change, so they can become more self-aware, overcome these biases, and embrace transformation.

- Build a safe environment in which people can fail and learn from their mistakes. This is key. This doesn't mean people are allowed to repeat the same failures over and over again. It means people are allowed to take risks and make mistakes. This encourages creativity, innovation, and an environment in which people can thrive. Encourage innovators to be 100 percent quick and 70 percent right. The gap can be fixed later.

- Encourage idea sharing and foster a safe, collaborative environment in which people can challenge on another's ideas in order to improve and iterate.

- Create an effective process for piloting new ideas.

- Shape a learning environment along the company's transformation, in which individuals are encouraged to continuously develop themselves with the intent to reach their full potential within the organization. This requires managers to commit to the development of their people aligned with the company's goals.

With a framework for change in place and a strong, proactive culture to support that framework, the strategies that will shape your company's future have a much stronger chance for long-term, sustainable success. It is this foundation and agile process that helps companies adapt to ever-changing markets and times while achieving still their current goals. It's what sets stellar leaders and companies apart from mediocre ones. Commit to the time and work it takes to create this foundation and you'll start to see amazing things happen.

## A Framework for Dynamic Stability

Now let's take a look at the framework. The three-dimensional conceptual graphic illustrates five levels of parallel-running program categories, which are plotted against the degree of innovation required on the y-axis, the time aspect on the x-axis, meant to show their continuity of development, and their estimated probability trend of future success on the z-axis.

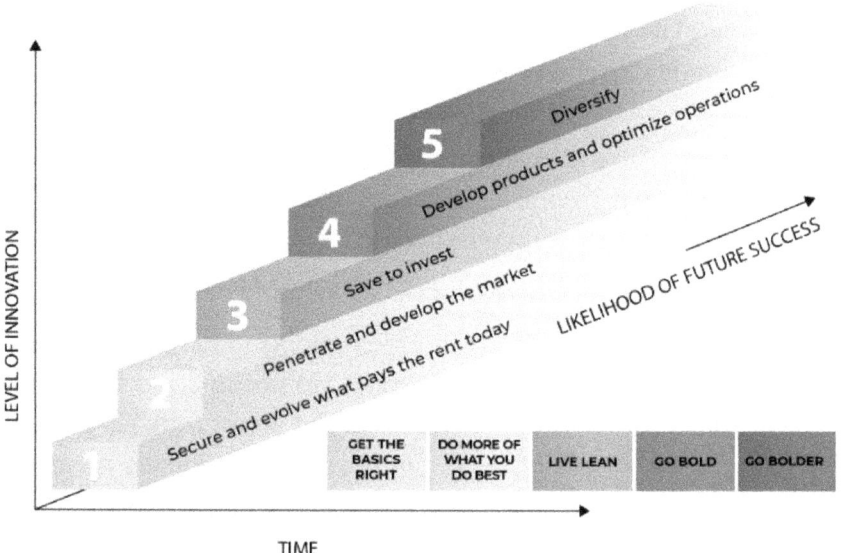

*Figure 3: Conceptual illustration of a dynamically stable business framework (The Mammoth in the Room, Nicolas Pokorny, 2024).*

## Level 1: GET THE BASICS RIGHT. Secure and evolve what pays the rent today.

Leaders often think business evolution starts by looking to the future. I fundamentally disagree. It starts with looking at what's happening right now in the business—with the basic activities, behaviors, culture, and processes that are paying the rent today. That's where leaders will find the true baseline to measure progress. This approach challenges leaders to truly understand their core business at any given point in time. Working on the basics means deeply understanding your customers—what they think and believe about the products or services you're selling, how they view your competition's offerings, etc. It means truly knowing *why* your company is performing the way it is today. In other words, it's not about knowing your current market share; it's about understanding *why* your market share is what it is. It's not about knowing your products' positioning, distribution, production cycle, operational excellence models, customer hit rate, and so on; it's about how all of this is seen by your customers and how and why it is contributing to your current success. It's about understanding how these things impact your company's profitability, growth, and all other important business metrics. If you don't know the basics of your current core business in the real world, you don't have a baseline from which to evolve or a clear understanding of what needs to happen next. If this is the case, you're going to make big mistakes.

Every business leader has made these mistakes at least once in their career, including me, of course. Here's a classic example of what can happen if you don't fully and clearly understand the present. A company discovers it is losing market share. Deeper analysis shows the competition has a higher face-to-face customer rate. The problem looks pretty straightforward, so everyone believes this is what is causing the loss of market share. The company decides it must increase its face-to-face hit rate with key customers to match and even surpass the competition. The logic behind this approach is that an increased hit rate will equal higher sales. Unfortunately, the leadership team hasn't studied whether the company's customer experience is actually positive. That's a big mistake, because guess what? The company's customer experience is a hot mess. So, instead of seeing higher sales, the increased face-to-face calls have the opposite result. Customers are turned off. In fact, the more successful the company is at hitting the identified metric—higher face-to-face hit rates—the more unhappy customers they have. Surprise! This causes their sales to shrink, not grow.

The leadership team's approach backfired because they didn't fully understand the problems causing their loss of market share. A simple sales force benchmarking exercise or deep dive into customer market research would have identified the real problem: a lack of sales force training. This is a common, real-world example of a company putting quantity (more face-to-face meetings) over quality (training their people to create better face-to-face customer experience). It's a backward approach that always backfires. But quantity solutions are typically easier to sell internally, so they often come first. Don't fall into this trap. *Quality must always lead quantity.* Ensure that your company is outstanding at the basics, the stuff that pays the rent, before trying to change anything else. Operational excellence is critical. That's why the first change in any business evolution must always be to fully understand the basics and get them right. If the basics—strategy, positioning, execution, production, distribution, and so on—aren't right today, you are absolutely not ready to think about tomorrow, because there might not be one.

## Level 2: DO MORE OF WHAT YOU DO BEST. Penetrate and develop the market.

Once you truly understand *why* things are the way they are today, and you have all the basics running smoothly, it's time to optimize your company's current core competencies—those things your company already does really well. Yes, more of that, please! Doing the right things more often will increase revenue with a low risk of failure.

In the product market matrix (see below), this means you focus on strategies to optimize your *market penetration* and embark on *market expansion*. What could possibly go wrong? Very little, because you know exactly what you are doing and why you are doing it. Your company is one of the best, or maybe even *the* best, in your market. If you can't do it, no one can.

The chart below offers a basic quadrant for market penetration and expansion. Though it's something we all study in business school, it's worth revisiting in the context of change and strategy. The chart has four quadrants in which one can find the strategies:

1.  Established products in an established market (market penetration).
2.  Established products in a new market (market development).
3.  New products in an established market (product development).
4.  New products in a new market (diversification).

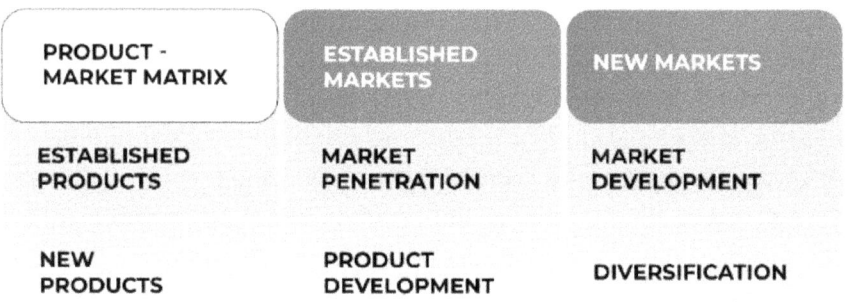

*Figure 4: Product-Market Matrix. The chart illustrates products and markets from a company internal perspective.*

In market penetration strategies, companies go deeper into the current customer base with existing products and services. You're looking for a segment you have not yet fully maximized. In this scenario, you might find ways to outperform your competition with new quantitative or qualitative promotional efforts, or both. I remember a situation where my company's product, a pharmaceutical specialty compound prescribed by specialty healthcare professionals, was the undisputed market leader. The only way to grow market share further was to go deeper into an established but rather peripheral customer segment that influenced prescribing this product to patients. They had the power to prescribe but did not usually do it because it was a specialty product. By involving this group more closely in our medical-marketing promotional efforts, we achieved a small but not insignificant boost of market share in the course of a year. Going into this campaign, we knew the chances for this strategy to be successful were very high because we understood our current customer segments, market, competition, and product very well. We had clarity around how all the basics were working, so we could optimize them with a low risk of failure. We knew all the moving parts at a very granular level. More importantly, we understood why the parts were moving the way they were moving. This allowed us to be surgical and precise in our efforts. We achieved higher market share without sacrificing profit margins, which is always the goal.

If the goal is to expand existing products from established markets into new markets (e.g., a new customer segment), a clear and granular understanding of the current state of affairs is equally important. It might be a bit riskier than the market penetration strategy, because in this case, you need to understand a new customer. But if you do the necessary research and understand the customer's way of decision-making, the upside in market share can be even higher than a pure market penetration strategy. A good example I came across recently is a European super fiber cloth manufacturer that took a staggered, incremental approach to both market penetration and expansion efforts. The payoff was huge. They were already successfully selling to enterprise customers in Europe, which used their products for commercial antibacterial cleaning in places like hospitals and hotels. They had also expanded into the consumer market for home-surface cleaning. In addition to product and space cleaning, their super fiber was also great for human self-care. But who wants to use a cleaning product on their skin? Impressively, this company successfully found a way to expand into the personal-care segment in Europe. When they intended to enter the US market, the leadership team had a decision to make—either enter both markets at the same time or expand more incrementally. They decided first to enter the US commercial cleaning market and hold off on the personal-care market. Only once they had figured out if their product worked well and would be successful in the US market would they consider expanding into the US personal-care segment. This gradual, intentional approach allows companies to continue expanding in a clear direction without upsetting the fundamentals of the current success.

When you sell more of what you're really good at to more customer segments, you're growing smart and not overextending the resources you have. Of course, there's always some friction with change. You have to figure out what resources will support the growth. This often means you'll need to learn how to do more with what you already have. This means working leaner.

## Level 3: LIVE LEAN. Save to invest.

Once a company is optimizing its market share and found new markets for established products, many leaders think it's time for business development strategies such as product development, in-licensing, or even diversification. Not so fast. There's one more step that needs to come first. You need to learn how to "live lean." For most businesses, profitability is the only currency that really counts. Profits are what fuel a company's ability to further develop and grow. If the company is a market leader, staying lean, flexible, and nimble to maximize profits generated by this leading market position is the first order of business. However, if the company is not a market leader or is struggling, the call to "live lean" is even more imperative, especially in tough economic times. According to a December 2022

McKinsey & Company blog post titled "What Is a Recession?" companies can prepare for economic downturns through "scenario planning, putting together a risk management strategy, ramping up your organization's agile processes, and ensuring your organization has rock-solid environmental, social, and governance (ESG) metrics."[71]

Leaders at profitable businesses realize that not everything they want to do can or should be done at the same time. They learn how to live lean and not waste resources. They invest their time and energy in those things that make a difference in the profitability of their company. If today's business can be done more efficiently, you will save precious resources that can be deployed for important initiatives—business development strategies, higher short-term shareholder returns, brand building, and so forth. To sustain success, businesses must stay lean, efficient, and effective at the same time. They must have the ability to reduce bottlenecks, make decisions quickly, and act opportunistically based on a clear understanding of their business basics.

Throughout my career, I've seen living lean create powerful outcomes. One team I worked on was able to replace a resource-heavy sales channel with a significantly more efficient one without losing market share. This innovative approach was based on our analysis that the product being promoted was an established market-share leader (and cash cow) that was familiar to all of our customers. We believed this product no longer needed the same cash, time, and resource-intensive sales effort to keep sales at the same level. We suggested that direct sales efforts could be scaled back and replaced with new and more innovative processes and sales efforts without losing market share. The approach worked. This freed up resources for other parts of the organization.

With another team, living lean was accomplished through a detour. Analysis showed that a new product had huge upside revenue potential if more resources could be provided. How does that lead to "living lean," you might ask? Well, in this case, investing in additional resources led to more revenue that not only outperformed the costs associated with that resource investment but also led to an increase in profitability of about 12 percent. This was achieved through an enormous economy-of-scale effect created by cross-functional, frontline sales support functions and processes. This was indeed a very innovative way to become leaner.

Unfortunately, most companies don't live lean. They invest in new roles, new departments, tons of new projects, and shiny new technologies because they *can*, not necessarily because they *should*. That's when things can go south. I once observed an organization going through a merger. The company that had been acquired needed an overhaul because the previous management had basically wrecked it. They had threatened employees, destroyed the company's culture, and driven the business into the ground. New capabilities, new knowledge, new processes, and new ways of working needed to be built quickly. It came down to the "culture eats strategy for breakfast" truism we discussed earlier in the book.

The company struggled for a long time until new management was brought in. With new leaders in charge, the company was off to a good start and was able to turn things around quickly—in less than 1.5 years—through a well-prepared and very well-managed revolutionary change process. Once a new, healthy, effective company culture emerged, business started to improve. This was all celebrated as an example of best practices across the wider global organization.

However, new headquarters' management misread the behavioral and cultural progress due to outstanding leadership for an outcome of better management and control mechanisms and processes. As a result of their misguided analysis, they built up huge control mechanisms and layers of bureaucracy across all departments and global locations. This immediately started to stifle the culture and caused backsliding, which in turn led to lower profitability. Instead of thriving, the company became vulnerable to takeovers. The new management team started out great but then did exactly what they should *not* have done. Unfortunately, it took this company almost a decade to recover and return to a workplace where people were proud to work.

A last point about living lean: save for rough times. Besides the obvious things that strong profits provide, like extra money to settle debts and pay dividends to shareholders, extra money in the bank also offers security and provides a buffer against future financial challenges. Bad things happen sometimes. This is just the way the world works. Extra money in the bank helps everyone sleep better. In the abovementioned McKinsey & Company article titled "What Is a Recession?" it is also discussed how preparation can help companies to build "systemic resilience" to weather the tough times, which are inevitable at some point in the future. And—not surprisingly—the companies who are most likely to succeed and might be even poised to thrive during a recession are businesses that "experience relatively steady demand for high-margin products, easily attract and retain talent, and have simple supply chains. From a financial perspective, they have strong balance sheets, low leverage, and lots of cash."

Always keep in mind, the most important benefit of higher profitability will always be the ability to allow companies to invest more in their future. Live lean, and continuously invent the future.

## Level 4: GO BOLD. Develop products and optimize operations.

While everything so far has been relatively low-risk—even when efforts are highly innovative—it's time to move into more ambitious and risky territory. The purpose of going bold is to build a bridge to a longer-term vision. As such, this step requires unique tactics—like developing and selling new products and services to your current customers. The reason this can be riskier than your market development is because your reputation is on the line. Imagine that your current clients think your products or services are simply perfect. While adding new products or services to your portfolio has an upside, because you're tapping into a well-known network of clients, there is a big risk. What if the new products or services are not as good as your current ones? That has potential for a negative spillover effect. You could alienate your currently satisfied customers with bad, insufficient, or immature products or services. This might shake their loyalty. I once witnessed a situation where a well-known and well-respected pharmaceutical company in the antibiotic space licensed a new antibiotic from another company in a business development deal. Unfortunately, the antibiotic developed by the other company did not meet the same standards in terms of efficacy, safety, and overall tolerability. In short, the antibiotic's entire benefit-risk profile sucked. Not only did this licensed antibiotic have very poor sales performance, it also had a negative spillover effect on the established product line. Customers felt that the company had lost its standing. Rest assured this endeavor did not last long. The new antibiotic was quickly removed from the market. Lesson learned. Companies must be very careful when they introduce new product lines to their existing customer base. This requires extensive testing and piloting to make sure there's something truly remarkable that's worth introducing to the company's loyal customer base.

In the same category, I want to put new and maybe revolutionary processes *to operationalize the business*. Imagine your customers are, as described above, happy with pretty much everything you do, and you decide to introduce a new process that makes it easier for your company to fulfill its customer requirements. Imagine you invest in a new order system but then, when the rubber hits the road, the system fails and your customers who are used to being served within a certain period of time have to wait 50 percent longer until their ordered service or product gets delivered, simply because the new system has its flaws and needs time until its up and running flawlessly. A situation like that can have a negative spillover effect on your current business and therefore needs to be avoided at all costs.

Meta's Galactica language model—probably an interlink between a new service and a new process—which failed only after a few days, is one example how difficult it can be to get product and process development right.[72]

Before we go even bolder, it's a good time to reflect on what we have done so far. We have introduced a way to gradually develop a business further in an active, strategically intentional evolutionary approach. You might be a few years into this journey, and your team, which you formed at the beginning, has gradually upped the risk while ensuring that your core business continues evolving at the same pace, or at least at the same pace as your competitors, with the intention to at least keep your market position. Make no mistake: to evolve your core business and keep it fit for the future over time takes as much innovative and creative thinking, piloting and failing, and cross-organizational learning as your development and expansion strategies.

While we touched on this already, it's worth mentioning again in the context of the framework: when people speak about innovation, they typically only talk about the far future—like the next big thing in 2030. Radical shifts, like switching a service fully to artificial intelligence or blockchain, or fully electric cars are some examples of ultimate innovations. But the future is also tomorrow, just around the corner. You need innovation to gradually improve your current business incrementally in the near future as well. Innovation is not only the next big leap. Sometimes it can be something small that improves your bottom line, efficiency, or user experience.

To future proof your business, you need to be strategic and intentional and tap into all your company's brainpower. The good news? If you do this consistently, you don't need the new and shiny breakthroughs. Unfortunately, you'd be amazed how few companies intentionally evolve incrementally over time. The companies that make continuous and sustainable evolution an overarching, company-wide goal are all too rare. But, wow, what a competitive advantage this can lead to.

## Level 5: GO BOLDER. Diversify.

So far, the framework we've explored is about minimizing risk and ensuring a high probability of success. Now we're finally ready to embark on higher-risk strategies like diversification and entering new markets with new products or services. Yes, these strategies are difficult and risky, but if done correctly, they can deliver a very strong competitive advantage. Business history shows those companies that got diversification right made a name for themselves: Amazon, Apple, IKEA, Disney, and Berkshire Hathaway, to name just a few. What are not often talked about are the risks involved, as well as those companies that failed. According to a research report from McKinsey & Company, "Growing Beyond the Core Business,"[73] of the 1,143 executives at companies with revenues above $500 million, only around a third were able to create value of more than 10 percent of their total business through diversification. In fact, 70 percent of businesses embarking on a diversification strategy found it created little value or underperformed. Another 10 percent stated that value was actually destroyed! So why would a company even consider diversification? The answer might surprise you. It's not to make short-term profit or improve the bottom line. This can be achieved without diversification. Diversification has a totally different goal: it prepares a company for the more distant future that's three, five, or seven years out. Diversification does not need to make money right away. It's about planting seeds for a future harvest. Too many of the executives interviewed by McKinsey & Company mistook transformation for instant revenue generation. When asked why they were expanding beyond their core businesses, 61 percent cited access to new profit pools. Not quite 50 percent said their company's diversification efforts were supposed to secure long-term growth. At least this group had the right mindset. But another 23 percent said they did it because they wanted to diversify risk and exposure to business cycles within their core industry. To me, that sounds like using gasoline to put out fire. If your core business is at risk, it does not seem intuitive to add another riskier strategy to "de-risk" the current one. If the basics of your business are not right, or the core competencies have not been optimized, your company is not ready for diversification.

What diversification is intended to do is proactively shape the future. It's meant to help the company's people acquire new skills, capabilities, and knowledge, as well help the company acquire new technology or R&D assets to tap into new markets with new products and services that optimize success. Does any of this sound like a quick revenue play? Of course it doesn't. Transformation is a long game that needs dedicated people, financial resources, and time. Diversifying a business is in itself risky, with new markets, new products, paradigm shifts, and predictions of a distant future. Who knows exactly how any of it will play out? If you then tie it to a business plan and expect it to pay for itself in two years and deliver a 7 percent yield in three, you're setting the diversification effort up for failure. This is why there's a 70 percent failure rate for diversification strategies. Not enough time is given for the diversification to fully evolve. This happens because people are not using the strategy correctly. Diversification will always fall victim to today's business. Therefore, the diversification effort needs to be detached from the current business and be handled differently. There should be no classic business plan, only a long-term plan—ideally with only trajectory ballpark numbers and time bounds attached to it, at least at the beginning. You can add precise quantitative measures, forecasts, profitability expectations, and so on once you understand the new business, once you have made your mistakes, and once you know exactly how to get the basics of that new strategy right. Only then does everything start over again. You might be thinking, *doesn't this contradict one of the major principles introduced at the beginning of the "On Strategy" section—that strategy must always be financial no matter what?* But there is no contradiction here. The decision to give a long-term diversification strategy the necessary time and resources it needs—and defer profitability expectations—is absolutely a strategic financial decision, and it's an important one for strategic growth.

If you and your people can commit to incremental, ongoing transformation according to the principles that are the foundation of the Dynamic Stability Business Framework, you have an excellent chance of becoming or staying a market leader in your industry. I can say this with confidence because I've seen it happen many times throughout my career. What I've sadly seen more of, however, are failed strategies—for all the reasons I've outlined in this chapter and throughout the book. Unprepared cultures, incomplete or erroneous data interpretation, or reactionary change-management strategies – in summary "*Strategy by opinion and who has them*" - all put a company at risk. Don't become a statistic. Do the foundational work to help your team and your company bake evolutionary transformation into their very DNA. Similar to life, business is like riding a bicycle. To keep your balance, you must keep moving. That's where it all starts, and in truth, that's where it all ends.

.

# Chapter 7

# Watch Out for Evolutionary Pitfalls, Biases, and Mismatches

As a leader, there's always a lot of pressure when it comes to creating and executing strategies. In the end, the buck often stops with you. In the "On People" section, we discussed how to build strong teams and improve ourselves and our people. In the "On Strategy" section so far, we've talked about how to implement strategies to help you and the organization reach key business goals and prepare for the future while keeping the business stable and growing in the here and now. In this chapter, we're going to focus on what it takes to lead teams through this balancing act—because it is a balancing act. There have been thousands of books written about leadership from a wide variety of angles—how to become a great leader, what great leadership looks like, and what the qualities of great leadership are, to name just a few. Characteristics like discipline, vision, fortitude, and ambition are often mentioned. But based on decades of research and my thirty years of professional experience, I'd like to spotlight a few different qualities leaders need to succeed: humility, empathy, self-awareness, and evolutionary consciousness. These are the characteristics that define great leadership in today's world.

In the introduction to the "On Strategy" section, I asked this multipronged question: What type of leader is capable of getting a reluctant group of humans to embrace change together in a coordinated fashion and in pursuit of a common goal? We explored the research of Mark van Vugt and Richard Ronay presented in their article "Evolutionary Psychology of Leadership: Theory, review and roadmap," which tackles the challenges leaders and organizations face due to mismatches between our evolutionary drivers and the demands of the modern business world. With the help of Vugt and Ronay, we also explored how evolutionary mismatches and pitfalls often compel organizations to choose the wrong leaders with the wrong qualities for the wrong reasons. This might even have happened to you, and now you're the person in charge of strategy and appointing the next group of leaders to execute it. You might be looking in the mirror and asking, "Am I fit for this job? Do I have what it takes?" What can you do to reverse your self-doubt? What can you do to become the leader who can get reluctant humans to embrace change together? As we explore this topic, I'd like you to look inward with an open mind. To succeed will require you to explore your own thinking and biases as well as the evolutionary pitfalls you're facing as the leader of others with their own sets of biases. You'll need to learn new ways of thinking and doing and unlearn old ways. In leadership, the past is always present, and what got you into your leadership position never guarantees success in your new leadership endeavor. Evolutionary leadership theory (ELT), which studies leadership from the perspective of evolutionary psychology, which applies the principles of evolutionary biology and behavioral ecology to better understand human psychology, tells us that traits are passed down through the generations, but over time, humans "face the risk of finding themselves perfectly equipped to deal with challenges that may no longer exists, and ill-equipped to deal with a host of new challenges . . . Because evolution through natural selection is mostly a slow, cumulative process, mismatches are particularly likely if environments undergo rapid change."[74] [75] [76] Again, a mammoth moment.

Business has undergone massive, rapid, and accelerating change since the start of the Industrial Revolution in 1750. As a result, today's leaders face many evolutionary pitfalls, including:

- False-positive and false-negative decision-making.
- The "as leader, I know all" bias.
- Wrong-sized groups (oversized).
- Mistaking followership for buy-in.
- The need for dominance.

I'll go into more detail about each of these pitfalls shortly, but they all have one thing in common: they exist because they served their purpose back in ancient times when life was about merely surviving, when small groups were organized around basic tasks, and when international conglomerates with complex global strategies didn't exist. If we were all still issuing memos with hieroglyphics on stone tablets, our evolutionary biases would still work in our favor. But since we're using smartphones to Slack our colleagues around the world, well, these ancient ways—ingrained in our DNA for hundreds of thousands of years—can cause problems and become a big roadblock for leaders and their teams. Worse yet, most of us aren't even aware these evolutionary biases are impacting how we lead, make decisions, and build and interact with our teams. That's why the first step is awareness. As I mentioned earlier, you'll need both self-awareness (to start noticing and correcting for your own biases) and evolutionary awareness (to understand the dynamic between your own evolutionary biases, those of the people you lead, and how this all plays out in groups). It's the dynamic between evolutionary biases in groups that influences behavior, so the problems and solutions are bigger than any one individual's biases. Let's dive into some of the biggest evolutionary pitfalls, biases, and mismatches we face as leaders.

## False-Positive and False-Negative Decision-Making

While in an earlier chapter of this "On strategy" section, I suggested decision science as appropriate instrument to deal with the evolutionary biases of human decision-making, it feels important to discuss this phenomenon specifically because it impacts businesses around the world every day, as it is deeply rooted in our evolution. Let me explain this phenomenon with an example from my own life. During one of my family's international moves to the US, while we were exploring our new home for the first time, my then fourteen-year-old son suddenly screamed at the top of his lungs from downstairs. We all rushed to help, only to find him standing at the top of the basement stairs, breathing heavily but looking very relieved. Apparently, he'd opened the basement door and stepped down into the darkness, where he'd mistaken a belt lying on the floor for a snake. We all laughed and went about our tour. But better this scenario than the opposite, right? He could have mistaken a snake for a belt and received a nasty bite. If the snake had been poisonous, he might have ended up in the hospital.

Why is my family's story important? Because it demonstrates (and we quote again Mark van Vugt and Richard Ronay) that all decision-making risks two possible errors—a false positive (assuming a false belief—a belt is a snake) or a false negative (failing to assume something that is true—a snake is a belt).[77] [78] These two errors often differ substantially in terms of cost. As I mentioned, falsely recognizing a belt as a snake might startle you, but grabbing a snake because you think it's a belt could send you to the hospital. This is exactly why our brains favor false positives (assuming a false belief—a belt is a snake). This false-positive bias keeps us safe. In humanity's early days, it was always wiser to make a false-positive mistake than a false-negative mistake. This bias helped us survive in dangerous, high-risk environments. As a result, we have evolved toward false-positive errors over false-negative errors. It's a form of loss aversion, which we discussed earlier. People tend to place a higher value on avoiding losses than on acquiring equivalent gains, which can lead to risk-averse decision-making.

How does this story and this bias impact us as leaders? Our evolutionary bias toward false positives has the potential to bite us in the bum every time we make a business decision (pun intended). In fact, such decision-making biases must always be considered as companies continuously evolve and test their strategic-risk tolerance. I've already cited some of the vast body of evidence suggesting that human decision-making is influenced by deeply ingrained evolutionary predispositions.[79] In the field of evolutionary psychology, researchers applied the framework of error management theory to understand how and why such cognitive biases evolved. Unfortunately, the evolutionary bias toward false positives causes business leaders to see snakes everywhere. In bigger companies, entire departments are charged with identifying potential threats that could cost the company money or market share. I watch it all the time. "We can't do that because we have a compliance constraint." "That's a great idea, but we've already evaluated the legal, commercial, and reputational risk and it's too high." "It's against our policies." When people or teams spot snakes in the grass, the company backs away from the initiative. It's why your new marketing strategy, sales campaign, production innovation, multichannel data collection, you name it, was stopped in its tracks. But 95 percent of the time, when decision-makers see snakes in the grass, it's actually just a belt lying on the floor. Over time, this false-positive bias can have a significant cost. Seeing snakes everywhere causes companies to become more and more conservative. And the bigger a company gets, the more it has to lose. There can be huge costs associated with inaction. Think of the stories I shared about Kodak failing to innovate in the middle of the digital revolution and Nokia's ill-fated software strategy. One multinational biopharmaceutical company in the early 2000s made this very error in their overarching company strategy and almost went bust.

After a while, the company's leadership gets tired of all the missed opportunities, so they course correct (or more often, course over-correct). A brave new management team is brought in to stop the nonsense of seeing so many snakes in the grass. The new team is given license to act. Common sense is abandoned. Real snakes in the grass are ignored in the name of progress. Everyone sees the snakes, but no one dares to mention them—unless they are willing to put their reputation on the line and risk demotion or even getting fired. Everyone tows the line because leadership is saying, "Go! Go! Go! There are no snakes!" This leads to false-negative decision errors. Think of SoftBank's loss of $14.4 billion as a result of their investment in WeWork, which only very recently emerged from bankruptcy.[80] Think how many snakes were ignored during that due diligence process! Other examples include Volkswagen's "emissiongate"[81] and Yahoo's bad bet on Tumblr in 2013.[82] These mistakes were driven by false-negative errors. They were bold decisions (though some folks might call them stupid) made with plenty of snakes in clear view, but everyone ignored them and suffered nasty bites as a result. In some cases, if the antivenom isn't administered fast enough, those bites can be lethal to a company.

Too many false positives and a company can become too cautious and fail to innovate. Too many false negatives when there are threats in clear view can also have devastating consequences for an organization. When you spot these tendencies as a leader, it's an opportunity to call out the mammoth in the room, build awareness of our evolutionary biases, and use that awareness to be more intentional in the decision-making process. This can prevent big mistakes and yield great opportunities.

## The "As Leader, I Know All" Bias

Another evolutionary bias that influences our decisions and behaviors every day is what I call the "as leader, I know all" bias. Who among us has not encountered the new department lead who brags about their performance and mastery of all topics during an interview? Who hasn't had a boss who talks the most in every meeting with his or her teams? Who hasn't seen a manager who constantly needs to school his or her people about how things "actually" work? Who has not experienced the boss who is always one-upping his direct reports? You know the type. And if we're being honest, we've all exhibited this behavior from time to time. Why? Because as leaders, we think we must know everything. But do we?

Where does this belief come from? It may very well be an evolutionary bias. As I've mentioned, early hunter-gatherer societies needed experts—and they didn't have a lot of choices back then. If the group needed a boat and you were the only boatbuilder around, you actually did have to know it all. But this isn't the case anymore. Today's "as leader, I know all" bias very likely stems from those ancient times and our expectation that leaders somehow must or should know more than the rest of us. As a result, leaders often feel compelled to show off their knowledge, accomplishments, and expertise. In my very early days in leadership, I felt that way. I was young and thought I had to prove I deserved the job. Add in the fact that everyone constantly expects solutions from leaders and you start to understand the "as leader, I know all" bias.

Additionally, ELT (evolutionary leadership theory) suggests that leaders are often selected for the very qualities that ultimately threaten their capacity for effective leadership—overconfidence, lack of self-awareness, defensiveness, and failure to learn from experience.[83] Such qualities might increase their chance for promotion, but these qualities may also make the leader more prone to a number of decision-making biases—including hindsight bias, illusion of control bias, confirmation bias, anchoring and adjustment bias, and escalating commitment bias. *Inc.* magazine had a great article on this topic. It was written by Gordon Tredgold, CEO of Leadership Principles, and opened with this memorable line: "There's nothing worse than working for a know-it-all boss." So true! But as Tredgold makes clear, this is more than just a morale problem. It has big implications for the company's culture and future. When people feel they have no voice, they don't stay committed. "When people are not committed," Tredgold continues, "they don't feel any ownership or accountability for the outcome. This means that if things start to go wrong or look like they are going to fail, they don't necessarily feel that it's their failure. And in the worst cases, that they don't believe that they have any responsibility to do anything about it, because it's not their plan, they are just following orders."[84]

Long story short, it doesn't have to be like that. Do not fall into this trap that as leader you need to be smarter than your team members and know everything. You don't. If you're talking more than you're listening or bragging about your own career and accomplishments rather than lauding those of your team members, you need to do a little self-reflection and correct this behavior. If you are feeling like you're the only one who can move things forward, it's time for a long look in the mirror. All that bravado might have landed you your current job, but it's not going to make you successful in that job. What *will* make you successful is listening, learning, and understanding the dynamics in the group you have inherited. Even when you know the solution to a problem, let your people identify the solution. It's your responsibility to empower your people with the skills they need to solve problems independent of you. So, don't try to be the smartest guy in the room. That's not your job description anymore. Making your people smarter is!

## Oversized Groups

In the opening of the "On Strategy" section, I noted that Walmart, as one of the biggest employers in the United States, has more than 2.1 million employees. This is an evolutionary mismatch example par excellence because we are a small-group species. As Vugt and Ronay describe in their research, humans evolved in small, hunter-gatherer societies that essentially acted like one big family: "Members knew each other, understood their interdependencies, and had a genetic investment in one another's fate.[85] [86] These groups were held together by kinship and norms of fairness and reciprocity, which require that individuals can depend on each other for assistance and will return in kind."[87]  Today, many people work in giant national and multinational corporations with tens of thousands, hundreds of thousands, or even millions of employees. Of course, there's a disconnect and dysfunction in organizations at this scale. How can there not be?

Leaders have tried to overcome the dilemma of large companies, which have become more popular because their size offers marketplace efficiencies. Amazon founder Jeff Bezos once famously said, "We try to create teams that are no larger than can be fed by two pizzas. We call that the two-pizza rule."[88] It's a great approach, but someone is still charged with leading all these small teams, likely through several layers of management. Even when a reasonable span of control is applied, it is inherently difficult to lead dozens, hundreds, or thousands of employees through multiple management layers. The communication of goals, knowledge, and processes becomes more and more complex—as does a leader's ability to gauge buy-in, commitment, and understanding from his or her team. Compare the potential for a disconnect in the modern corporate environment to the small hunter-gatherer band societies of our ancestors. They are worlds apart. Now, add in remote work, business travel between offices, and time zone and cultural differences, as well as the multiple departments and management layers of the modern-day work world, and well, authentic and effective communication becomes nearly impossible. Our brains haven't evolved quickly enough to handle the new demands or scale of today's vast, global business world. That's why silo thinking, miscommunication, and misunderstandings can quickly spread across modern organizations. The symptoms of this broken model show up in all sorts of places—dysfunctional teams, high employee turnover, flawed measurements and processes, slow growth, underperformance, misguided pay structures and incentives as highlighted for example in a report by Statista in 2022, which "estimated that the CEO-to-worker compensation ratio was 344.3 in the United States. This indicates that, on average, CEOs received more than 344 times the annual average salary of production and non-supervisory workers in the key industry of their firm".[89] Really…?!? And I could go on with examples like that, but I guess you get my point.

The only way to address this evolutionary mismatch is with a strong, healthy culture. If your organization's culture is high functioning, then your eight direct reports or ten project-group peers may be able carry your strategic vision through their span of control and influence. But this only happens in adaptive, human-centric cultures that recognize our evolutionary need for "kinship and norms of fairness and reciprocity." You can't expect alignment around strategic goals without intentional and proactive shaping and nurturing of this type of culture. Without this, focus and commitment problems will continue to fester and spread. Left unchecked, the deterioration can be catastrophic. Imagine a silo mentality around a key strategy that is closely tied to the company's financials. At the highest levels of the organization, the outcomes of this strategy are measured carefully against useful financial KPIs and metrics. But at the department level, the understanding of the strategy and measurement of its success are murky. Additionally, the department's sub-strategies are not fully aligned with leadership's strategy—though no one realizes this. In fact, nobody is seeing the big disconnect through all the layers of management. Nobody realizes the culture's silo mentality is causing any issues. But because the culture is unhealthy, small problems grow into bigger ones for several years. Now the company is dealing with a crisis. Finally forced to confront all the problems, the CEO and his or her leadership team dive deep. They start to connect the dots and pull the plug on costly sub-strategies that are losing the company money and market share. And this is the best-case scenario. In worst-case scenarios, the company is forced to lay off droves of employees to stay afloat. These scenarios haven't been invented out of thin air. They happen all the time. Most of us have seen it with our own eyes.

## Mistaking Followership for Buy-In

We talk so much about leadership and write books about it. But rarely does anyone write about followership. It's a bit like commenting on a tennis match purely from one side. As we've already said, where there are leaders, there must be followers.[90] To a large extent, strong leadership is about creating an effective leadership-followership relationship. This seems straightforward, but many leaders confuse followership with buy-in, which is a big mistake. Before we can explore this important distinction, we need to fully understand the different types of leadership and followership relationships and how they can set the stage for success or failure.

The Leadership-Followership Matrix shows the different situations leaders can find themselves in when trying to develop strategy. The matrix is designed to help leaders honestly evaluate their situation and analyze the true state of their leadership-followership relationship. This is important because it is ultimately what makes or breaks strategies—and businesses. The Leadership-Followership Matrix has four quadrants, with leadership tracked on the y-axis and follower-ship tracked on the x-axis. The higher the leadership arrow goes on the y-axis, the stronger the leadership behavior. The farther to the right followership goes on the x-axis, the stronger the followership behavior. In order to demonstrate what these quadrants look like in the real world, I've added a list of scenarios—all of which I've witnessed at least once in my career, most multiple times. Leaders need to be able to spot these scenarios quickly, and the Leadership-Followership Matrix can help.

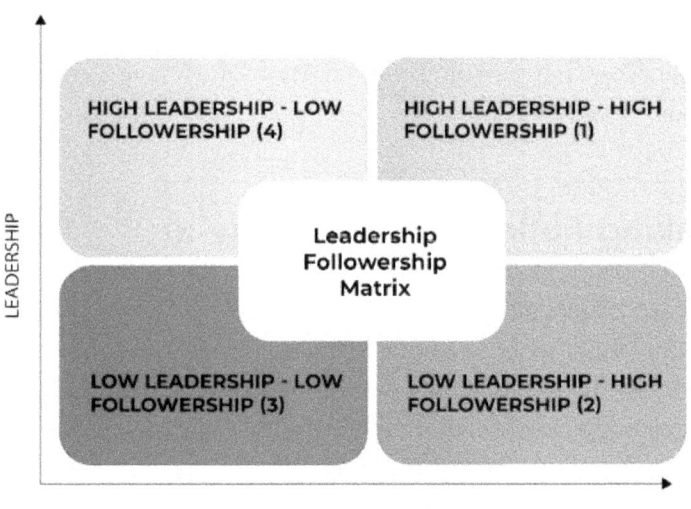

Figure 5: Leadership-Followership Matrix. The numbers in the quadrants are for orienta-tion purposes only and do not represent a certain order of sequence (The Mammoth in the Room, Nicolas Pokorny, 2024).

If as a leader and team, **you find yourself in the upper-right quadrant (1)**, where there is high leadership and high followership, this may be an environment for the following positive or negative scenarios:

## Positive Scenarios:

- This is a real team that has stormed, normed, and is now performing. They know what to do, which is a strong sign that the team is moving in the right direction.

- There is strong alignment between the leader and the team, as well as a no-nonsense attitude. Conversations about how to align on strategy happen well before a strategy sees the light of day.

- Team members are fearless and comfortable taking risks in a collaborative, "bring it on" environment.

## Negative Scenarios:

- The leader has established a culture of fear while constantly telling everyone, "Just be honest with me." No one believes this leader will accept honest feedback, so everyone shuts up and follows along rather than challenge the boss.

- The leader has established an unhealthy culture and is surrounded by folks who try to please him or her in return for favors. Pandering comments like, "You make a great point, leader x," or "I totally agree, leader y," are not only common, they are the norm.

- A young or inexperienced team believes their overconfident leader knows everything and they follow blindly. Team members never challenge their leader and have no clue that he or she could be executing a flawed strategy or guiding them toward a cliff.

**If you find yourself in lower-right quadrant (2)**, where leadership is low but followership is high, the following positive or negative scenarios could be in play:

## Positive Scenarios:

- The leader is new and in the process of establishing authority. He or she is treading lightly for a while in their new role.

- A dedicated and not very experienced team believes in the leader and is prepared to support him or her with the time and energy necessary to establish a strong leadership-followership relationship.

- A highly experienced team knows what to do and is willing to coach a new or non-established leader.

## Negative Scenarios:

- A new or non-established leader is struggling to establish an effective leadership-followership relationship.

- A team overpowers the leader. There's an imbalance in the leadership-followership relationship that is not in the leader's favor. Despite the leader's ineffectiveness, the team tries to keep the external picture positive to ensure the weak leader stays in place—avoiding change either because the team members like being in control or they're complacent. This power play reigns even though a leadership change might be better for the leader, the team, and the organization.

- A laissez-faire leader or management-by-exception and (potentially) reckless leader has built a culture of fear in which his or her employees don't dare to challenge anything.

**If you find yourself in the lower-left quadrant (3)**, where there is low leadership and low followership, the following positive or negative scenarios could be happening:

## Positive Scenarios:

- A very new team has just been formed and is still finding its footing. The leadership-followership relationship is still evolving.

- A team is faced with an unfamiliar new challenge and is struggling but still learning. Despite the challenges, the future looks bright for this team.

- A strong but inexperienced leader with good intentions needs external support to orient an inexperienced team and get them off the ground. The potential for establishing a healthy, effective leadership-followership relationship is still high but needs some assistance.

## Negative Scenarios:

- The leader is negligent and has built a dysfunctional culture where no one wants to work. As a result, everyone on the team is struggling.

- A laissez-faire leader has allowed complacency to set in. Everyone on the team has given up, and no one cares about moving the company's strategy forward. Everyone is just doing what they want to do instead of what they should be doing.

- A new leader is facing destructive behavior from team members who oppose or won't give the new leader a chance to develop a healthy leadership-followership relationship. This happens often when a team is "mourning" the exit of a former leader, which was potentially an involuntary departure.

**If you find yourself in upper-left quadrant (4)**, where leadership is high and followership is low, the following scenarios are possible:

**Positive Scenarios:**

- The leader is not yet fully established. He or she is on the right track but still needs to convince some skeptical team members.

- The leader has been put in charge of a hopeful new team in the storming phase and is trying to lead from the front.

- The leader has been put in charge of a high-performing, efficient team with a healthy conflict and challenge culture. There is respect, but this team does not follow their leaders blindly when they think they might be headed in the wrong direction.

**Negative Scenarios:**

- A leader is leading from the front but doesn't recognize the team is having trouble keeping up or is feeling left behind.

- A capable and hopeful leader has been put in charge of a destructive, oppositional team. There are frequent, unhealthy clashes.

- A new leader has been put in charge of a traumatized team or a team that is still mourning the loss of a beloved former leader. Team members can no longer see the company's strategic vision and have lost their bearings. This scenario can happen to either well-intended leaders or reckless, non-inspiring leaders.

As you assess in which quadrant you and your team might currently reside, keep in mind that the key is to do so with your eyes wide open. In bigger teams, it makes sense to do this exercise anonymously and on the team level so you can look in aggregate at the result where the team, leader, and followers place themselves. If you can objectively understand where you are today, you'll have a much better chance to behave in a manner that will move you and your team toward a healthier and more effective leadership-followership relationship tomorrow. This, in turn, will create a strong foundation for alignment around strategic initiatives. When the leadership-followership bond is healthy and productive, followership typically does equal buy-in; when it is not, followership has nothing to do with buy-in. *This* is the crucial distinction you must be able to make as a leader. It requires a clear-eyed view of the realities surrounding this important relationship. Also, keep in mind that this relationship can change based on the task or topic, but as long as the culture is healthy, this is absolutely okay. A true "every hand's a winner, every hand's a loser" assessment will prevent you from mistaking followership for buy-in. Believe me, I've fallen into this trap myself and watched others do the same. This assessment shouldn't be taken lightly or rushed, because if you don't get it right, you'll continue to operate based on an illusion. This wastes time, energy, and talent. You'll keep wondering why your team or teams all agree to implement a strategy but never get it done. It's much better to understand the relationship and fix it if necessary, so you can all function together at your highest level. That's when you'll be capable of leading a group of humans to embrace change together in a coordinated fashion and in pursuit of a common goal—and *that* is the most important strategy of all because it makes everything else possible.

## The Quest for Dominance

When President Vladimir Putin of Russia invaded Ukraine in 2022, the world watched in horror. Everyone wondered, "Why did he do this? Why impose so much destruction and loss of life?" We all wanted answers. It didn't take long for the global media to start profiling Putin and help us understand his thinking. On March 31, 2022, CNBC reported what was a common theme in the Western press: "President Vladimir Putin's immense power looks like it might now be a key weakness for the Russian leader, with those around him seemingly too scared to tell him the truth, or to question his rationale or strategy when it comes to Russia's invasion of Ukraine. 'Putin systematically got rid of people who could have challenged him, leaving only the most loyal and fearful ones,' Anton Barbashin, a Russian political analyst and editorial director of the journal Riddle, told CNBC . . ."[91]

Putin's "leadership" of his country—and you'll understand the quotes around that word later in the chapter—is a perfect example of our fifth evolutionary bias: the quest for dominance. It rarely ends well but continues to be an approach people in positions of influence and power use to get their way. Does evolution provide any clues as to why we humans still consider this approach to be a viable option? Yes, it does. Vugt and Ronay's research suggests that our quest for dominance results from the competition for scarce resources that decided our survival in the early days of our species. They note that our "closest (no human primate) genetic relatives all live in groups characterized by dominance and power hierarchies." There are exceptions, like the pygmy chimpanzee that developed a matriarchal system, which we discussed in the "On People" section, but even this species is not entirely free of violence.[92]

So, in general, most nonhuman primates rule with dominance—either intragroup or intergroup, or both. They establish power and hold on to it. But unlike our genetic relatives, we have always lived in highly cooperative groups, which requires something more than mere dominance, as Vugt and Ronay note:

> To be able to live and function in highly cooperative groups requires mechanisms and procedures for coordinating social activities, sharing resources, keeping groups together, and leveraging the benefits of participatory decision-making.[93] This phase of evolution caused attenuation of the traditional dominance hierarchy, replacing it with a decision-making hierarchy benefiting the entire group rather than a few powerful individuals (van Vugt, Hogan, et al., 2008).

Dominance was thus replaced by leadership, whereby individuals voluntarily coordinated their actions and goals
with people they believed could help them achieve group
goals. In return, individual leaders competed with each other to attract followers but this competition was based more
on prestige and respect than on dominance and coercion.
This move away from dominance to prestige-based leadership was a pivotal step in human evolution . . .

This does not mean we got rid of the quest for dominance. We just
learned how to use it selectively or even hide it. But this strong bias
is still present. In fact, it's everywhere, influencing our behaviors in
everyday life, business, politics, and culture. People still try to dominate—be it in a conversation, negotiation, project, the media, or in
groups, in companies, in countries, and even across the world. How
does this need for dominance manifest in companies? Sometimes
subtly, like the boss who emails a task with a Monday deadline
over the weekend or late on Friday afternoon. Of course, the email
has the obligatory message: "You are not expected to look at this
over the weekend." Both parties know you will. Or worse, your boss
inserts a disclaimer in the bottom of the email that says, "I'm just
sending this now. I don't expect any of you to work on this outside
working hours." Really? Then why the late notice and the Monday
deadline? There are also those managers who are always late to their
own meetings while subordinates are expected to be punctual. And
there's the boss who lets the full onsite team, which has prepared a
stellar presentation, wait for twenty minutes. Upon arrival, he or she
says, "Sorry, I got stuck in a meeting." Of course, this leader would
never show such disrespect to his or her management team. There's
also the leader who lets a request from management simmer for
days and then suddenly asks team members for feedback that needs
to be delivered in twenty-four hours. I could go on, but you get
the idea. Most of the time, these leaders don't even realize they're
exploiting their employees. They just look at them as subordinates

because they can, especially if they work in a culture that tolerates, or even cultivates, this type of unhealthy leadership dominance.

"Dominance is still part of our ancient primate heritage and there is plenty of evidence from traditional and modern societies that leaders will coerce followers if they believe they can get away with it (Betzig, 1993; Padilla et al., 2007)," write Vugt and Ronay. "To get your way as a leader it is much easier to dominate than to convince people to follow you." Modern and ancient history are filled with stories demonstrating the enduring legacy of this destructive approach. But make no mistake, dominance does not equal effective leadership. At its worst, dominance manifests in the following ways: undermining or getting rid of rivals, using fear to control people and get them to do what you want them to do without consideration for whether it is in the best interest of the team or company; blaming others for your shortcomings and failures to deflect criticism, and pitting people against each other to create chaos and weaken team members so you can hold on to power. Leaders who choose dominance over authentic leadership are destructive. Just like know-it-all leaders, dominant leaders need to stop and take a close look in the mirror. If you feel you might fall into this category, pursue leadership training and mentoring because you're currently not doing yourself, your team, or your company any favors.

## Human Behavior Drives Strategy

Every single strategy decision since the beginning of time has been a manifestation of the behavior of the humans behind this decision. Research makes clear that human behavior is strongly influenced by evolutionary wiring that moves at a much slower pace than today's ever-changing, tech-enabled world. However, if we become more self-aware, and more cognizant of our evolutionary drivers and biases, we at least have a shot at keeping up. We also become better, more effective leaders. That's the simple but powerful message of this chapter—a message that has a profound and ongoing impact on the teams and companies we serve. In any particular business context, management's strategy successes or failures are an expression of human behavior gone right or wrong. What we need to regularly ask ourselves as leaders is why did one initiative prevail while another was derailed? In my experience, negative outcomes don't correlate with a lack of skills, knowledge, or experience. The answer is not a workshop, conference, or yet another credential or advanced degree. The real problem is a lack of understanding of human behavior and the forces that drive it. To be successful at work, we humans—whether leaders or not—must interact effectively in a highly interdependent social system that we call a company. Not only is that interdependent social system spiraling through times and changing markets, but it's carrying the past with it—all the individual and collective wiring, history, and behaviors of all the humans in that social system. Yep, there are a lot of passengers on this fast-moving journey, and they all bring a lot of baggage. And, yes, you're the leader, but you're also one of the passengers. So maybe it's time to make sure you're all moving in the right direction and in the same direction—evolutionary baggage and all.

# Chapter 8

# Be Political

You only find two kinds of people in companies: those with plans and those without plans. Most of the time, the people without plans work for the people with them. This leaves us with only two choices: work without plans and support others who have plans or work with plans and live up to your potential. In the first scenario, we accept that others will tell us what to do and how to do it. If you're comfortable with this, you can make a good living and have a nice life. I know many people who are fine with following others. They don't want to be in charge, which is totally okay. But it is rare for someone without plans to become a leader, so that life path won't be open to you. In the second scenario, you assume leadership roles and strive to get your plans across the finish line. This takes a unique set of skills because every plan has two components: the plan itself and the execution of that plan. Without successful execution, a plan can't become reality, so it's not much of a plan. Many people can create plans but don't know how to execute. So, if you want to be a successful leader, you must be able to do both.

Execution is actually more difficult than planning because a leader can create a plan on their own, but it's impossible to execute on most plans alone. It takes a team and a network to get it through. I don't care how good you think your plan is, nothing gets implemented without a supporting network—and building that network takes skill. Even in small organizations, leaders encounter different opinions, opposing plans, and conflicting interests. Success requires the support of key decision-makers. It only takes one important player to nix a project or favor another one. Effective stakeholder management is crucial. That means mapping out all key stakeholders, identifying team members to approach each of them, and planning out how and when this approach will happen. If you skip this step, chances are very high that your plan will end up on the very crowded shelf of "not implemented but beautiful PowerPoint" plans. How do you avoid this? Get political. I know we're all taught that "being political" is taboo. People say, "I don't like company politics!" But company politics are a reality, and as a leader, you must learn to play the game. Have doubts? Hear me out. Being political has a negative connotation because we think of it as a form of exploitation—something dominant leaders use to keep others under control. But being political for the right reasons—to support and defend a key business plan or strategy, your people, or all of the above—is an important skill that successful leaders master. To give your strategy a fighting chance to see daylight, you need allies to push it through. So, prepare to be political.

I recently had a conversation with a mentee of mine who just landed a very nice leadership role. During our conversation about her first months in the new job, she said, "One thing I love is there are no politics." She spoke of an environment in which everyone was transparent, and no one had an agenda outside of achieving the goal at hand. "No one plays any political games."

I remember thinking, *As nice as that sounds, she's wrong!* As she was only a few weeks into the new company, I didn't want to curb her enthusiasm, so I held my thoughts for another conversation but still gave her this advice: "It's great that you feel like this at the moment, but stay observant. You're new to this company and still learning about their culture." Inside, though, my brain was processing the lessons I'd learned a thousand times in my career and the evolutionary science we've explored throughout this book: human beings compete to maximize their individual fitness. This is our key biological driver. When we come together to enjoy the benefits of the group—like better odds of survival and greater economic opportunities—we seek a delicate balance between meeting our own needs and supporting the needs of the group. Given these facts, do any of us really believe that all the people working in a company to make a living and support their families will do so without any lobbying, partisanship, power plays, or self-promotion? No way! This is why company politics will always exist. There is nothing inherently bad about this state of affairs. Company politics are nothing more than the dynamic of influencing others through different power structures—hierarchies, professional titles, long-term relationships, success, networks, official programs, etc. Every department, level, team, function, process, budget, and problem is influenced by company politics. They exist everywhere and impact everything. This isn't good or bad, it just is! Whether you like it or not, it's how we humans tick. You fight this strong evolutionary reality at your own risk, because company politics happen all around you, every day, with or without you. You can ignore this reality and let corporate politics shape your professional experience and plans, or you can start learning how to be political and shape your future.

I do want to make one important thing clear before we move on: company politics do not impede great organizational cultures. A healthy corporate culture exists when employees support the company's vision and strategy while nurturing their own individual dreams and goals. Individuality is the glue of any great team, department, or organization. But even in the greatest company cultures, individuals compete for limited resources—budgets, people, leadership titles, time, and so forth. Leadership's handling of this complex dance between the needs of the individual and the group ultimately defines the company's culture for better or for worse. But the existence of company politics does not necessarily equal a toxic corporate culture where leaders have succumbed to the evolutionary pitfalls we discussed earlier in this section. Look for a healthy corporate culture where being political means supporting the company's vision and strategy while nurturing your own dreams and goals. Now, let's dive into what being political looks like in the real world.

## Build Relationships When the Sun Is Shining

The best way to manage strategic stakeholders when you need to implement a plan is by utilizing an existing network. If you try to build a network when you need it, you're already too late. Networks must be built when they are *not* needed.

For some people, this is a difficult concept, including me during the early days of my career. When I was young, I was always worried about being "productive"—getting the job done and doing it right. Back then, my rookie brain told me that networking carried the opportunity cost of not utilizing the very same minute for doing something "productive." I still remember my first sales manager advising, "Nicolas, whenever you are at headquarters, always talk to the CFO. He is very respected, knows everyone, and pulls the strings behind the scenes. Talk to him on regular basis and he will give you advice and help you if your ideas are good." I am embarrassed to share that I followed this great advice exactly zero times. Back then, my brain told me, "Talking to the CFO steals your time, Nicolas. You should be working on the next big thing that everyone will want because it will be so brilliant." You can imagine my surprise—and the lessons I learned—when my projects did not receive the attention I thought they deserved.

I'll say it again: no matter how good a plan is, *nothing gets implemented without a supporting network.* Here's how my more evolved professional brain thinks these days: taking time to build a strong network is one of the most productive things you can do as an aspiring or current leader. There are small, quick opportunities to build your network every day: grab a cup of coffee with a colleague, have a ten-minute conversation in the hallway to update someone on a project and get his or her opinion, introduce one colleague to another, pat someone on the back for a job well done, thank a colleague who supported you, lend your support to someone who needs a hand or feedback, or make a positive comment in a meeting about another person's project that you find interesting and worth pursuing. You need to build relationships and networks when you *don't* need them in order to tap into those networks when you *do* need them. In other words, build your network when the sun is shining.

Good relationships take time and effort to develop. With consistent nurturing over time, individual relationships grow into strong professional networks across multiple management levels and functions. The people in these networks are the ones who will support you when it counts. This is why networking is a very important leadership skill. You can't be a successful leader alone, and you can't implement a plan—no matter how good—by yourself. As Zig Ziglar famously said, "You can have everything in life you want if you will just help enough other people get what they want."

## Map and Follow the Power Grid

A lot has been written about the influencers, decision-makers, power brokers, alliances, networks, and so on that shape a company's power structure—or power grid, as I call it. These are the movers and shakers who make things happen and point the company toward the best people and ideas. They can make or break a leader. Since networking takes time, you need to be strategic. This means understanding your company's power grid. Map out the power grid, so you can build the right network of people who will support you and energize your plan when it counts.

Many people think corporate power structures are mapped by titles, but that's not always the case. Power grids are often not that straightforward. For example, most people believe the general manager, who leads the company, also makes the ultimate decisions. That's true most of the time, but not always. Another belief is that senior employees have better opportunities to shape policies and processes than newer employees. That's often true, but again not always. Hallmark departments like sales, marketing, and finance—and their leaders—are usually guiding company decisions and strategies. But is it the department lead or senior marketing manager who owns all the external connections? Or is it the sales manager who negotiates the prices with significant accounts? Just because you can't see these structures up front does not mean they are not there.

As a young professional, my lack of interest in networking revealed my naivete. It showed that I had not started asking questions about my company's power grid. I didn't think about how internal politics and professional agendas could impact my ability to achieve my goals, much less about how the company's power grid drove decision-making and strategy. But I know this now. Today, as a result of my hard-earned wisdom, I have quite a sophisticated understanding of power grids. I have held around twenty different roles within four companies across five countries and two continents, and I can tell you emphatically that it's a company's *unofficial* power structures that you need to understand. They are always more important than the official ones. How do you uncover and map these unofficial power grids? Regularly to talk to people. Ask questions and listen. Read between the lines. Try to understand the history between people and teams. Then start to draw out the relationships. That's right, I'm talking about drawing a physical map. I don't know how often I have done this on the whiteboards at my office and at home. Get creative and use colors! Try to evaluate relationships and track interactions until you have a complete power grid. There's your road map to success.

As a leader, if you're willing to do your homework and map out your company's *real* power grid—the one driven by relationships, not titles—the dividends can be huge. Whatever is thrown at you, good or bad, you'll know the real decision-makers who can support you. I've seen it all in my career: a general manager steered by a former general manager's agenda, business departments only able to make decisions at the discretion of the finance department, business unit leaders beholden to other unit leaders rather than their own department's priorities, new general managers used as marionettes by headquarters and turning against their own teams to save their own hide, etc. These realities are neither good nor bad, they are just realities. You do not need to like it, you just need to learn how to navigate it effectively. Your hard work will pay off when your plans, ideas, projects, and budgets become a reality and your team's hard work pays off and is rewarded.

## Keep Friends Close and Enemies Closer

This famous piece of advice comes from Sun Tzu, whom we've already quoted liberally in these pages. His classic book, *The Art of War*, is highly recommended reading. It's a strategic masterpiece, with lessons applicable for life and business. But is Sun Tzu really advising us to stay closer to our enemies than our friends? Not exactly. What he means is keep a closer eye on potential troublemakers. Be alert to their activities and alliances. If someone is making your life difficult, undermining your authority, or opposing you at every turn, well, Sun Tzu would advise you to watch them closely, as they may cause more trouble for you soon.

Ignoring or avoiding troublemakers is a big mistake. I've watched too many professionals suffer the consequences, including myself. It's better to understand their agendas to ensure you're not caught off guard. Always keep the people likely to undermine you and your team's efforts on your radar. Your gut normally tells you who these people are. Chances are good that these folks are also on other people's watch lists. Your networking will help you speak to others about the usual suspects worth monitoring.

It's not just your enemies who require attention. I've created my own version of Sun Tzu's saying: "Keep your friends close and your stake-holders closer." We've already discussed how important it is to understand your company's true power grid and network with the right decision-makers. The health of your professional network can make or break you. Don't neglect the people who can help you achieve your goals. These stakeholders might not be your best friends or people you want to hang out with all the time, but don't neglect your relationship with them. Don't turn a potential supporter into a potential opponent just because you forget to keep them close.

## Never Play Dirty Until Necessary

Once your networking and stakeholder-management skills have been honed, you'll start to enjoy the benefits of your growing network. The full benefits will unfold over time as your tenure lengthens and you become part of the power structures that guide your company's decision-making. People will begin to seek out your opinion and feedback more often. If your role in the company grows, you might be thought of as a critical "co-owner" of some of the most important power structures in your company.

Of course, with greater power comes greater responsibility. Having political power and using it correctly—at the right time and for the right causes—are two very different things. Too often over the course of my career, I've encountered people who have misused their connection to the power grid for their own benefit. The outcome is always unpleasant. So, in general, always tell yourself: "Don't play dirty." Once power becomes too one-sided, everyone suffers. "Power is dangerous," said Ragnar Lothbrok, king of the Swedes in the TV series *Vikings*. "It corrupts the best and attracts the worst."

So where do you draw the line as a leader? Sometimes it's simply more expedient or easier to wield your power instead of going through normal channels. Power can make things easier, and that is the danger. For example, you're in a time crunch to solve a big problem and you believe you have the best solution. To keep things in motion, you shut down the thoughts and ideas of your colleagues because you can. This might solve the immediate problem quickly, but you have probably damaged your credibility as a fair leader, which can have long-term consequences for the culture of your teams. That's never good. Maybe you start ignoring feedback or quit being grateful for the support of your team. This can also have a negative impact on your team's culture and performance. I myself had moments earlier in my career when I did not use my power and influence wisely. But then I learned I should never take out more from my environment than I am prepared to give back—a great truism from nature. Luckily, while I was learning and reflecting, I became a stronger leader, and I handle things differently now. I allow myself to be more sensitive and more considerate. I listen more and push back more selectively and intentionally. My growth as a leader has created a stronger culture on the teams I manage. As a result, we have better outcomes. King Ragnar Lothbrok's words come to mind again: "Power is only given to those who are prepared to lower themselves to pick it up."

Sometimes, though, situations arise that compel you to use your power in a more forceful way. This can happen when you have to stand up to people who are abusing their power. As you see these situations, you might ask yourself, *How can I tell whether someone is abusing their power? How can I tell if I'm using my power fairly?* These are legitimate and tricky questions, but the fact that you're asking them is a good sign. The best way I know how to respond is this: you'll know it when you see it! When powerful people take advantage of those with less status, that's abuse of power. When people display destructive behavior because they know they are protected, that's abuse of power. When people play dirty and risk the good reputation of their company, that's abuse of power. I have experienced all of these scenarios, and none of them are pretty. I've learned how to confront such abuses of power when I see them in order to protect my team and the company. In these cases, which are rare, I become willing to wield my own power—and play dirty. If you have a good reputation and you need to turn on the heat in these types of situations—to protect your people or the company—people will understand and continue to respect you. My advice: stay humble and grounded as your power grows. Sometimes, however, your network will expect you to play a different game in order to achieve a particular goal. But in general, my advice stays the same: never play dirty until necessary.

## Hit Hard and Early

When dealing with people and problems, it is almost always best to compromise. Approach issues with an "everyone wins so everyone can thrive" philosophy. Even when a compromise is not possible, it is usually best to agree to disagree and move on—at least until it's not. If someone seriously oversteps (e.g., reckless behavior toward peers or subordinates), don't hold back. Hit hard and early. Stop bad behavior in its tracks. Draw a very clear line in the sand so the message to this person is unmistakable: do not go one step further. People actually appreciate the clarity. If there's a gray area, things will get worse. Don't let this happen. Cement your reputation as a leader who never abuses his or her power in normal circumstances but wields power like a mighty sword when necessary for the good of the team and company. This will rarely be necessary, but at some point, you will be tested—and everyone will be watching to see whether you stand your ground. Be ready and remain resolved. I've seen the benefits; I've also seen the negative outcomes when a leader fails to draw a clear line in the sand. Don't make this mistake. Hit hard and early.

## Conclusion

Most people believe that companies, departments, and units—and the visions, strategies, people, and cultures that support them—fail or don't achieve their optimal outcomes because their employees, in their collective knowledge, capabilities, and skills, don't know how to develop a competitive strategy.

I disagree! Businesses fail for very simple reasons. Most of the time, it's the human factor that gets in between a winning strategy and its successful execution and optimal outcome. Why does this happen so often? Because most leaders don't understand human nature and the role of evolution in daily human behavior and group dynamics. Acquire this knowledge and you will set yourself, your team, and your company up for sustainable high performance. If you ignore the realities of evolution, simple problems will grow into mounting failures and crises. Unfortunately, most of these simple truths must be learned in the real world on a leadership journey, where you are constantly striving to achieve dynamic stability between the often competing priorities of today and tomorrow. It's not an easy balancing act. Mastering this balancing act requires continuous learning, experimentation, and discipline.

All businesses are human systems. If you are charged with leading a human system, you must manage your own evolutionary heritage and biases as well as those of everyone else in your human system. This might seem daunting, but acquiring this knowledge and these skills offers a key competitive advantage. We know the ultimate strategic goal of every business leader is to help their company successfully navigate through markets and times. They must make sure the business performs successfully not only today but also tomorrow and five to ten years into the future—and beyond. This only works if you are continuously working on the company's transformation, which is not easy because the future always falls victim to day-to-day urgencies. The only way to overcome this problem is to build a culture of continuous transformation. Given humanity's evolutionary bias against change, this is indeed a mighty task for every business leader. Remember, too, that structure always follows strategy and that nothing gets implemented without a supporting network. You need to build and nurture this network when the sun is shining, so it's ready when you need it. If power and culture are not well managed, even good plans can get sidetracked by selfish humans who want to take more out of the system than they are prepared to put in, trying to take advantage of what great teams were able to develop and nurture. There are always competing teams, plans, and priorities—no matter how healthy a corporate culture is. Don't ignore the natural evolutionary tension between the individual and the group. It's a delicate dance, and it's one reason that it's necessary to be political. Most importantly, as you grow and learn to become a strong, effective leader, your power and influence will rise. Use these hard-earned gifts wisely, intentionally, and from a place of humility and gratefulness.

# Section III

# On Implementation

*If you spend too much time thinking about a thing, you'll never get it done.*

—*Bruce Lee*

# Overview

Throughout history, the biggest names in business have been champions of relentless execution. Edison, Ford, Bezos, Gates, Jobs, among others, are so famous I don't even have to mention their first names. Yes, they all had, or still have, amazing ideas and vision, but the reason they became famous was because they knew how to get #$@% done! They knew how to execute, how to implement their ideas and vision. Steve Jobs famously said, *"To me, ideas are worth nothing unless executed. They are just a multiplier. Execution is worth millions."* There is nothing, and I mean nothing, more important in business than implementation. In *The 8th Habit: From Effectiveness to Greatness*, bestselling author and leadership coach Stephen R. Covey, drove home the point when he wrote, *"Most leaders would agree that they'd be better off having an average strategy with superb execution than a superb strategy with poor execution. Those who execute always have the upper hand."*[94]

*But you can't build the foundation for a high-performance implementation culture on the fly while you're executing. That's like starting to teach your child to drive at 70 mph on the highway instead in a parking lot at 5 mph. It's irresponsible and dangerous. People are likely to get hurt. The same is true for high-performance implementation cultures. You start small, train, and build. This way, when execution*

*demands that everyone move at warp speed, the whole team is pre-*
*pared to meet the challenge. This is why the first section of this book*
*is all about building strong teams and supporting talented people.*

## Becoming an Implementation Champion

To master implementation, you must be lightning fast, outrageously
brave, and continuously flexible. Mastery, as you well know, is not a
destination but an ongoing part of your leadership journey. Learning
and polishing all of these skills must be an everyday routine if you
want to get to the top and stay there. What do I mean by this? Well,
an implementation champion permanently lives outside his or her
comfort zone—and encourages everyone else to do the same. They
also fully understand that strategy must sometimes be bent to accomplish the goal. Implementation is where the rubber hits the road,
so there must be a willingness to defend and fight for necessary
adaptation to keep things moving forward--whether this means
fighting key stakeholders at headquarters or showing customer-fac-
ing entities why a shift is necessary. You can't be rigid and become
an implementation champion.

Implementation champions are also strong, organized, and calm
communicators. They start by articulating clear goals and then create
a framework to help everyone navigate what's ahead. This is foundational to success. Heading into the implementation phase, the team
must align around a framework with clear responsibilities, processes,
frequency of tasks, and key data to be tracked. Then, once you're
actively executing, it's important to remain calm and collected, even
if events aren't unfolding as expected. These communication traits
and strategies are the hallmark of a true implementation champion.

If you're new to implementation leadership, there can be a lot to
learn and juggle in a high-stakes environment. Don't worry, the
steep learning curve will be worth the effort. Keep refining your skills

and growing. In the first leadership role in which I was responsible for implementation through multiple layers, I learned more about business and myself on one project than I had in all my other professional roles combined. Because I was not prepared for this mighty task when I took the role, I had to learn, grow, fail, and adapt quickly on the job—otherwise, I wouldn't have had the slightest chance of surviving, let alone succeeding. In this role, and in many other similar leadership roles that came afterward, I achieved quantum leaps in my personal and professional development. More importantly, the teams I was honored to lead achieved quantum leaps as well. The way each team conducted business was transformed by the demands of successful implementation. This work fundamentally changed how I, as well as my teams, approached and conducted business.

## The Opposite of Effective Implementation

For every company that does implementation well, there are dozens that do it poorly. I've survived many flawed implementation cultures over the course of my career. It's not fun. I vividly remember one large multinational company where the managers wanted to see an impact from the implementation of an initiative after just a few days—a goal they did not clearly communicate. In fact, no one on the implementation team understood the problems, requirements, or goals. It was complete pandemonium. This was early in my career, and I was only a few weeks into a new company and leadership role at the time. At first, after my manager screamed at me for not showing results in a few days, I thought the lack of impact was my problem. *I must not understand what's going on*, I told myself. *I'll push myself and my team harder.*

But others also seem confused. It quickly became clear that the problem was much bigger than me. When I look back at the situation now, it's easy to spot the leadership issue. The company had not built an effective implementation culture, yet top leaders expected everyone at every level of the team to act like they knew what they were supposed to be doing. Such a disconnect sounds unbelievable in a big company, but it happens all the time! Everyone agrees that they're checking the data, but the communication is nonspecific as to which data and how often. There are many assumptions made, which is a big mistake. In my particular situation, everyone *thought* they were implementing, and everyone *said* they were implementing, but nothing was happening. There was confusion and no sense of urgency. People can only execute effectively when they understand the goal, have been given clear expectations from their leaders, and know how success will be measured. Absolute clarity is the master skill of leadership. None of this was happening in the environment in which I worked at that time. Additionally, leadership's expectations were unrealistic. While some leading indicators can show early success, most big implementation projects take time to deliver the desired lasting results. Why? Because most of the time, implementation requires behavior change (for example, a shift in customer perspective or a change in employee behavior). These things don't change overnight. Everything about that implementation—or lack of implementation—took a toll on the company. As I recall, it took quite a long time to course correct and get the company moving in the right direction again.

# Chapter 9

# A Culture of Implementation Excellence

Let's talk about the characteristics that distinguish a culture of implementation excellence. Lou Gerstner, former chairman and CEO of IBM, once said, "I came to see, in my time at IBM, that culture isn't just one aspect of the game—it *is* the game. In the end, an organization is nothing more than the collective capacity of its people to create value." So true! As we know, value may be conceived at the strategy stage, but it's delivered as a result of expert implementation. With this in mind, what are the traits of a culture of implementation excellence? Here's my list, based on decades of experience. The people who are part of a culture of implementation excellence possess the following characteristics.

# They Have a Deep Sense of Urgency

In a culture of implementation excellence, steps to achieve the goal are taken immediately. Things are discussed and agreed upon in a meeting, and as people are walking out of that meeting, they are already on their phones or sending emails to their teams or customers. They start executing instantly. With implementation, the goal is always *100 percent quick, 70 percent right, and the rest can be fixed later! You will never have 100 percent of the information you need to make your implementation decisions, so don't get frozen in place waiting for something that won't arrive. The perfect market conditions, the perfect agreement, the perfect competitor situation, and so forth don't exist. You must do your best with what you know in the time you're given.* If you work in an environment in which people frequently say things like, "I'll look into this and come back to you" or "Let's take this offline," but then don't come back within an hour to take the next step, there's no sense of urgency. If you see people agreeing on next steps but failing to execute quickly, you're not working in a culture of implementation. You might ask, "What if my team has a heavy workload? Isn't that a fair reason to move more slowly?" No, it's not. Teams with a strong sense for urgency can prioritize and reprioritize according to the needs of the moment. If leadership doesn't quickly come back with clear direction on how to prioritize those needs, the team will keep executing anyway. If leadership comes back in due time with guidance on where to focus their energy and which tasks to finish first, they're on it immediately. But they're not shy about sharing realities. They'll tell you frankly that if you want something done right now, something else will need to wait. Teams with a deep sense of urgency know how to juggle multiple duties amid shifting timelines and priorities. They align on the direction so they can stay in motion and always have a backup plan to handle changes in a dynamic environment.

# They Are Effective Tightrope Walkers

By its very nature, implementation is a precarious process. The experience is much like a circus performer walking a tightrope. The stakes are high. To get from point A to point B up there, you can't just walk on autopilot in a straight line at an even pace. Continuous rebalancing, weight shifting, and a laser-like focus are required. Sometimes a tightrope walker slows for a moment to steady themselves; other times, they speed up to reach the other side more quickly. An unexpected breeze might cause them to stop momentarily to regain their balance. It's a complex skill that can't be taught in a classroom. It must be learned by doing. Imagine telling a team member to be relentless and persevere in pursuit of a goal while at the same time telling them they must be able to let go or pause if the opportunity costs get too high. Imagine telling these same team members to stick to the plan but be flexible enough to pivot and deviate from it if another way opens up that looks more promising and be comfortable with the related uncertainty. It requires one to be calm and collected but also vigilant and flexible—just like a tightrope walker. It might seem like a contradiction, but one must be both rigid and fluid. As Bruce Lee famously said, "Be water, my friend." Water takes the shape of anything you put it in. It adapts fluidly (pun intended) to any situation and still remains a powerful force of nature. In my career, I've observed that the greatest implementers have this intangible mix of attributes. The best implementers know how to walk the tightrope to get from point A to point B while taking in stride all the little adjustments required along the way. These types of implementers always achieve the highest market share. Their team members always earn the highest bonuses and are the first to get promoted. Why? Because they always deliver. They always get the job done because they know how to walk the tightrope effectively.

## They Strive to Be Fearless and Resilient

Implementation excellence also requires teams to be fearless and resilient. They have the courage to take intelligent risks and recover quickly when things go wrong. What does intelligent risk look like? It's hypothesizing quickly based on the information and data currently available. During implementation phases where speed matters (e.g., sales campaigns, events), teams rarely have all the information and data they need. The urgency to implement precludes time for in-depth research, so people have to gather what they can quickly and do back-of-the-envelope calculations about possible outcomes. That's what intelligent risk-taking looks like in the real world—weighing the pros and cons based on available business intelligence, planning, personal experience, and the gut feeling that comes with it. You must also weigh your willingness to take risks and decide whether the odds are in your favor. When you feel the probability of success is high, you take the risk. Intelligent risk-taking is crucial in implementation scenarios where one needs to be quick and bold. One-hundred-percent guarantees don't exist in this type of environment. One needs to be light-footed, able to improvise, and think outside the box. This takes a degree of fearlessness. When the intelligent risk doesn't pan out as hoped, that's when resilience is required. There is no time to wallow in failure during the implementation phase. You have to pick yourself up, learn what you can from the situation, and move on to the next challenge.

## They Have a Strong Desire to Win

Everyone wants to win. But people in high-performing implementation cultures want to win so badly they take it personally if they don't. It's about excellence and achievement. Be it taking market share from a competitor, getting a big contract signed, reaching the highest quota, or doing something else beneficial to support the team, top implementers try harder, push further, and do everything possible to achieve the goal and win. Defeat is personal. It hurts! I know because that's how I feel if I don't reach an implementation goal. I'll definitely go the extra mile to avoid disappointment. I still remember an 8:00 p.m. phone call with one of my sales managers while I was driving the 150 miles home after a few long days at the HQ office. The call was supposed to be a brief check-in about a long-held, underperforming account, but the two of us were determined to turn things around. We discussed, planned, agreed, disagreed, threw things away, and built up new approaches. Our ten-minute call turned into almost two hours of lively conversation. I ended up driving right past my home to my sales manager's house at around 10:00 p.m. that night. We dove deeper into the problem and fleshed out the best approach. When I left at around 2:00 a.m., we had agreed on a battle plan that we'd start to implement the next business day, which was only a few hours away. Tired but determined, we began implementation. Within twenty-four hours, the first positive feedback about the account started coming in. We'd taken this problem, this failure, personally and now a win was on the horizon.

## They Are Relentlessly Disciplined

What does it mean to be relentlessly disciplined? It's the mindset of doers who are constantly preparing and empowering themselves to achieve more. This takes relentless, not occasional, discipline. The word *discipline* is from the Latin word *disciplina*, which means "instruction and training." It is derived from the root word *discere*, which means "to learn." So relentless discipline is about continuous training and learning. For leaders, this means you and your team are always preparing for the next big challenge—even when things are slow or quiet. You're always enriching your mindset, honing your skills, and learning new things that can help everyone succeed. When the next implementation challenge hits, everyone is stronger, more prepared, and ready to take on the biggest challenge yet. Relentlessly disciplined people accept that every action is a learning opportunity to get better. They accept that whatever you do, how-ever successful the outcome might have been, if you did it again you would do something different because you have learned what would have made the outcome even better. Relentlessly disciplined people never say, "If I could, I'd do it all over again." For them, that seems stupid—like living every day twice without learning or improving. Relentlessly disciplined people never stop optimizing, practicing, and improving.

In my experience, these five characteristics are the hallmarks of a culture of implementation excellence. They indicate that your team is ready to act boldly in the real world, adjust to constantly changing realities, and urgently problem solve their way around roadblocks. While strategy and planning offer time to reflect and adjust, they are primarily theoretical exercises. Implementation is about achiev-ing goals in the real world while the company continues to move forward through changing markets and times. It's nothing like the controlled environment of the conference room where the strategy and planning took place. With implementation, there will *always* be surprises and changing realities that require adjustments on the fly. If your team doesn't possess all five necessary characteristics for implementation excellence, take the necessary time to work on the weak areas before your next implementation. These characteristics form the foundation of your success. You and your team need to be in top form. As Mike Tyson, considered one of the most contro-versial but also one of the greatest heavyweight boxers of all time, once said, "Everyone has a plan until they get punched in the face." Build a strong foundation with these five characteristics so you're prepared for the inevitable surprise punches that await you in almost any implementation.

# Chapter 10

# The Hard Facts of Implementation

Things will go haywire at some point during your implementation phase. This is just the way it is. But this doesn't mean you can skip the strategy and planning phases. In 1957, President Dwight D. Eisenhower told attendees of the National Defense Executive Reserve Conference, "Plans are worthless, but planning is everything." All implementers know and accept this truth. Everyone needs a plan, even if the real world is going to punch holes in it. As we've already discussed, nothing *ever* goes according to plan during implementation. If it does, your plan is not ambitious enough, and you're not moving fast enough. The plan is the road map, but it's your team's implementation culture that shapes how people react when the first boulder falls and blocks the road. The plan tells you the destination and the best path to get there, but careful scenario planning and your implementation culture determine when and how everyone arrives at that destination in the face of inevitable challenges. The plan shows you what it looks like to win in theory, but your team's implementation culture determines whether you win or lose in the real world. Rigorous planning that allows you and your team to work through all possible scenarios prepares implementers to adapt quickly when reality hits during the actual implementation phase. That's why Eisenhower's observation about planning is spot-on.

So, how do you enable and nurture a high-performance implementation culture? There are several practices and tactics I suggest every leader adopt. Each is simple but not always easy to practice in the middle of the implementation phase's typical speed and chaos. No matter. These practices serve as a crucial foundation, so model relentless discipline by following them.

## Measure, Measure, Measure!

After establishing the implementation objective(s), the next step should be to agree on very specific data sets that will be used to measure how the implementation is going. These data sets should be simple to understand, easy to track, and most importantly, relevant to the goal of the implementation. In other words, the data should provide clear guidance to the team so they can draw conclusions and enhance performance quickly. While this may sound straightforward, it's not necessarily easy to achieve. Here are a few cardinal mistakes I've seen around data and measurement:

- **Not enough data.** This is typically due to budget constraints and happens most often at smaller companies or in smaller departments. This means the implementation team is operating in the dark and will struggle to measure whether the implementation is moving forward effectively.

- **Too much data.** (Or too many types of data or data sources.) This is often a big company issue. Different people bring different data sources to the table, but no one sorts out which ones really matter. The weight of managing too much data can bog down the implementation process.

- **Misalignment.** Misalignment around what data to measure is very common in big companies. It can happen for a variety of reasons, but here's one popular scenario. The implementation planning begins and there's plenty of discussion around whether certain sources of data are too early, leading, or lagging, whether popular data sources are relevant or useless, and whether those sources are precise or imprecise. Teams spend days or weeks on these discussions. However, when the implementation begins, no one has finished the conversation, so different people choose different data sources to measure progress. There's a complete lack of alignment around which data sources matter and why. This scenario might sound unlikely, but I see it happen all the time. Someone needs to weigh all the opinions, draw some conclusions, communicate those conclusions, and make sure everyone is on board despite their differing opinions. All too often, this last, crucial step doesn't happen. Misalignment around how to measure the effectiveness of an implementation can cause big problems and plenty of confusion.

- **Shifting data.** This can happen when someone decides to change which data sources matter or when an entire company or department decides to change the data vendor for economy of scale reasons. The outcome? Confusion as everyone tries to get their bearings because the data from different sources are largely incompatible. In my junior years, I tried to solve such incompatibility issues myself. Today, having painfully worked through such transitions many times, I task the data vendor with this job. They need to come up with the reasons and assumptions around why certain data points look different, make more sense, or are comparable. My advice is to not waste your personal time on incompatibility. You're paying data vendors and sources a lot of money to do this for you.

When it comes to measurement and data sources, four very important ground rules come in very handy. **Rule one:** choose only a few relevant key performance indicators that actually measure the effectiveness of what you're trying to execute. Less is more! **Rule two:** these data sets should be easy to understand and easy to track. **Rule three:** include your team in the decision-making process and make sure everyone aligns around precisely what will be measured, how it will be measured and when, and in what context the data will be used to guide the implementation. Once there is agreement on these three things, **rule four** kicks in: everyone needs to shake hands and commit without further discussion or second-guessing, no matter what the data looks like when it comes in.

## Hurry Up and Get It 70 Percent Right

"If everything seems under control, you are just not going fast enough," world champion F1 race car driver Mario Andretti famously said. I agree! As I've mentioned, you'll never have all the information you need to make perfect decisions. You'll never have all the planning time you want to prepare for every scenario. And you definitely will never have perfect conditions during implementation. It would be wonderful, but it's not how the business world works. However, these realities don't give you a pass. As a leader, you are still expected to execute—and fast. So, what's a leader to do? It's worth highlighting my mantra again: *"100 percent quick, 70 percent right, and the rest we fix later!"* This is a ratio I use to weigh my decisions in an environment in which there is constant tension between getting it right and getting it done. When I'm leading a team through a strategy implementation, this ratio is always on my mind.

*You might be wondering, How can someone admit that they are striving to get only 70 percent right? That means you get three out of ten tries wrong. Put that way, the ratio sounds terribly risky. It appears to be sacrificing quality and accuracy for speed. I understand how someone might arrive at this conclusion, but it's not true. In fact, the exact opposite occurs in the real world. You maintain your speed but become more accurate and deliver higher quality solutions. How can this be? Because you and your team will learn much more by executing in the real world than by theorizing about the real world on a whiteboard in some conference room somewhere. And the faster you go in the real world, the more you learn. As long as you and your people are open to listening and responding to what is happening during an implementation, then doing will be the best teacher.*

*Since we talked about driving and cars earlier, let's look at a real-world example of this ratio at work in the Formula One (F1) world. For those not familiar with this sport, it is one of the world's most challenging and daring automobile sports. Only about twenty drivers are allowed to compete each year. It's the pinnacle of motorsports for the fastest and best drivers, who are supported by the most skilled and innovative car designers and engineers in the world. Now get this: While during the COVID-19 pandemic, the UK-based F1 teams and their brilliant technicians were quarantined and sitting idle in their car factories, thousands of people were dying due to the unfortunate lack of available ventilators. There are seven F1 teams in the UK, and they were all told to do nothing because the F1 season was canceled, and no one was allowed to work on the cars. Frustrated, the F1 teams offered their skills to the UK's National Health Service (NHS). They wanted to help build desperately needed ventilators for their fellow countrymen. One of the technician teams attended an NHS briefing to learn how these lifesaving ventilators needed to work. The technicians left the meeting, and thirty-six hours later, the first prototype was ready—not thirty-six days, but thirty-six hours! Now that's speed! Was it perfect? No, but they could continue fine-tuning. The need for ventilators far outweighed the need for perfection. With a prototype in hand, the seven F1 teams quickly combined efforts and started Project Pitlane.*[95] *Instead of sitting around, these talented engineers became part of a UK-wide effort to manufacture and deliver respiratory devices to support the national need. This bold decision-making and just-do-it attitude helped save many lives. This is what my mantra, "100 percent quick, 70 percent right, and the rest we fix later," looks like in the real world.*

In my own experience, working in leadership positions for large, multinational corporations, I have implemented complex strategies with the teams I was honored to work with many, many times. We've juggled multiple management layers, diverse teams and departments, competing agendas, seemingly impossible deadlines, a smorgasbord of personalities, numerous time zones, and different cultures and geographic locations to implement important strategies for companies. Our successes always emanated from exhaustive planning for multiple scenarios balanced with a need to move as quickly as possible. This is why the best approach was *"100 percent quick, 70 percent right, and fix the rest later!"* We always planned for what could go wrong—but even then, everyone knows the world is full of surprises that no one could possibly imagine. Just think about how the global pandemic derailed business strategies! Even so, planning to the best of our abilities enabled us to be somewhat prepared, stay highly responsive, and improvise while still moving forward at the speed of light. The teams we built learned how to solve complicated problems on the fly. Over the years, I've worked hard to demonstrate for my teams the implementation behaviors and characteristics that are necessary to achieve shared goals as quickly as possible. They've always known that, for me, excellence and winning are personal. We rose to the occasion in an environment of mutual respect so that we could all win. That's what diligent planning and a high-performance implementation culture looks like when aligned. I understand that moving quickly without complete information or a feeling of complete control makes many people feel uncomfortable. I tell my teams to lean into this discomfort, to get comfortable with the uncomfortable because it's necessary. Do you think a tightrope walker ever feels comfortable? Doubtful. Discomfort is part of the experience of moving quickly from point A to point B when the stakes are high. I've always believed in the famous saying, "If your dreams don't scare you, they're not big enough." Dream bigger and get comfortable with being uncomfortable. This is how you will achieve great things in work and life.

## Practice, Practice, Practice!

*Throughout my early career, most of which was spent in sales, I was always told not to memorize my sales pitch. "Memorizing your sales pitch is stupid," my managers and colleagues told me. "It kills creativity." I didn't care. I only felt confident if I knew the pitch by heart. And I really mean by heart—to an extent that somebody could wake me up at 3:00 a.m. and I would be able to deliver it flawlessly. Now, after many years of success, not only as a sales rep and small-team leader but as the head of sales or commercial at various large multinationals, I know my approach was right. No matter what people say, it works, trust me—and not just in sales. Think about the last time you spoke with someone who knew his or her product inside out. Impressive! Consider that person on your team who is super savvy on all data, evidence, and competitor comparisons. Irreplaceable! And we all know those people who can tell a good story flawlessly from beginning to end. They are mesmerizing. These people are so prepared they can handle any objection, command any room, or close any deal. They are winners. Thoroughly preparing allows the content to become second nature so you can concentrate on body language, voice, and all the additional intangibles that make your message even more powerful than the words you are speaking.* Those without the perfect elevator pitch don't reach the second floor, they don't see the door to the executive suite open, they don't typically get the sale, and they rarely reach their goals. When you and your team are preparing for an implementation phase, practice, practice, and practice some more! It will make all the difference. There's a wonderful quote from McKayla Maroney, an American gymnast who was a member of the gold-winning American women's gymnastics team dubbed the Fierce Five at the 2012 Summer Olympics in London. She said, "Do not practice till you get it right, practice till you cannot get it wrong." *Yes!*

## Incentivize Excellence

High-performance implementers are always pursuing their next big win. They're driven and expect to be rewarded in a number of ways for embracing the speed and excellence required during implementation. A well-designed incentive program ensures they'll stay engaged and stay with the team. Remember, top talent is always being wooed by other departments and companies. Make sure you're wooing them back with effective incentives. In addition to all the plans, performance indicators, reporting requirements, and other managerial tools shaping your team's behavior, an effective incentive system can foster the healthy, high-performance dynamic you want to see during an implementation. I stress this because I've seen so much damage caused by ineffective bonus and incentive systems. Some are downright demotivating, and in worst case scenarios, they can kill entire implementation operations.

High-performance implementers like to see their impact quickly. They don't appreciate personal targets or goals they can only achieve on a quarterly or annual basis. If you want a team to move quickly while maintaining excellence, you need to give them clear, short-term targets worth chasing. I've been a long-distance athlete all my life, and even I break the race down into sections in order to measure my progress and stay motivated. Imagine telling an elite marathon runner that they can't look at their watch until the race is over. They'd be devastated. It would throw off their race. So why would you tell your implementation stars that they will only be measured once a year? It doesn't make sense. It doesn't set them up for success. They want to keep continuously improving, pushing themselves, and competing as often as possible.

Your top implementers usually don't have a lot of additional time or bandwidth; they're too busy executing and achieving goals. So, like your general communications, keep your incentives short and simple. If you can't explain them on a napkin, they're probably overly complicated and require too much data and too much time.

*It's important to respect your implementation stars even if the business plans are wrong (they always are). Exact targets are rarely hit right out of the gate. Through financial gymnastics, you might achieve your aggregate targets, but on the account, geographic area, or individual level, you will always be off. Since your aggregate results will sometimes deviate positively or negatively from your targets, you always need to incentivize your superstars—well, nearly always. Even when you are way off plan, you will achieve something mainly because of your best people. A lot of incentive systems do not recognize this fact. In situations where the environment changes to an extent that your forecast is way off track, the last thing you need is to demotivate your superstars. On the contrary, experience has shown me that the performance gap between your best and midlevel people will always stay the same. Your best people will always inspire your midlevel people to do better. This is a reality I've watched unfold over and over again. Hence, when you increase the performance of your top 10 percent, your superstars, they will pull up your midlevel performers, who represent 60–80 percent of your team. There will always be a bottom 10 percent that will not be able to follow, and that's okay. You might think about separation for this group—internally and sometimes externally. Healthy turnover shows that you are getting better as an organization. The point is that your superstars are always going to drive performance no matter what goes wrong with the business plan. This means your incentive system always needs to be set up in a way that rewards your superstars and reminds them frequently why they work for you.*

*At its heart, implementation is an epic quest, and one way to incentivize high performers, who love to see immediate impact, is to gamify this quest. This fun approach can also help relieve tension in the middle of a stressful implementation. Why not make achieving the next goal in the epic quest a hunting game with a great prize for the one who achieves it first? In one of my earlier sales roles, I invented a system like this that offered monthly and quarterly opportunities to "win" something—from dinner to show vouchers, to affordable weekend getaways, to monetary amounts, you name it. Mostly, this was about bragging rights for the winner. It was healthy, competitive, and highly supportive, all at the same time. What a blast we had due to the fun team dynamic it created. Everyone waited eagerly for the monthly list to come out to see who had won. It was fun and effective!*

*I know these approaches work because I've tried them. It is about finding a good mixture to support your high-performance implementation team. Of course, all incentive systems and approaches have to meet company guidelines. Believe me, I get that and have lived with such corporate limitations for decades. But most of the time, if you get creative, you can find fun, supportive, and effective levers that foster an intrinsically motivating environment and destress and inspire your team while getting leadership to sign off on your approach. If you have a strong track record of leading high-performance teams through successful implementations, that's the most powerful lever of all.*

# Chapter 11

# Implementation Soft Skills

To support your team through the tough realities of implementation, you need soft skills. Your attitude, flexibility, and ability to inspire and support your people are all crucial. Any effort that enables you to create an effective and harmonious environment for your team is a soft skill worth learning. If this is not an area of strength for you, get some coaching or training, because soft skills are more important than ever. In this chapter, we'll discuss some of the soft skills I consider most important during implementation. And yes, they are all important in any business situation, but specifically in the implementation phase you can measure if you get it right.

## Appreciate, Recognize, and Mentor

By expecting your team to execute with speed, determination, agility, and excellence, you're compelling them to put themselves in a continuous state of discomfort for an extended period of time. You're asking them to execute without all the facts and to remain calm and collected but still vigilant as they walk a tightrope to help you get from point A to point B while the stakes are very high. It's a lot, so thank them frequently and publicly. Make sure their efforts are recognized individually, among their peers, and department- or company-wide. Mentor them through the tough times. Each one is a professional development opportunity during which you can share wisdom and comfort. You can also create opportunities for team members *to share the tough situations they've dealt with and the solutions they came up with to overcome their toughest challenges. You can even ask a few people to share how they turned a failure into a pivotal learning moment that helped them grow professionally (you're allowed to go first, by the way). Not only will this help people feel proud, recognized, and valued, but there will also be a positive side effect, as organizational knowledge grows exponentially through these shared moments. Additionally, people will become less concerned about what is being asked of them. A we're-all-in-this-together feeling will help them stay strong through implementation challenges. The speed, risks, accountability, and improvisation you are asking of them will feel more normalized and shared, rather than lonely and frightening.*

## Be Open and Accessible

*Communication is key during the implementation phase. You are in charge of creating these channels at different levels. This can be everything from individual or group emails, to weekly or sometimes even daily in-person or virtual meetings for small teams, to whole-team training or pep sessions. Whatever it takes to help people feel heard, appreciated, and supported, it's your job to create these channels, make sure people know how to use them, and ensure people feel that you are open and accessible when they need you. Because implementation may demand long hours and travel, I recommend you set up all these communication channels before the implementation begins so you can be available when your people need you. Many leaders say they'll be available, but then they don't show up when needed. Ever had a manager tell you to call them anytime, but when you did, he or she didn't pick up? Later, they told you they just didn't see your call come in. Do yourself a favor and never be one of those managers. I always tell the teams I lead, "When you think something is so important you need to call me after hours or on the weekend, don't hesitate—just call me, and I'll pick up." I follow through on that promise. This is what every leader should say and do for their people normally, but specifically during implementation phases.*

## Acknowledge the Fear

As we outlined in the "On People" section, never believe that you're the only one who experiences fear when riding the roller coaster that is business in today's fast-paced, ever-changing environment. Everyone experiences fear, no matter what bravado they show in public. The question is, how do we cope with it? What I've found to be a useful approach in these situations is to ask yourself a single question: *"What would I do if I had no fear?"* It brings instant clarity. *I wouldn't be paralyzed; I would act. I would keep moving toward the goal, even though the road ahead would be treacherous.* The interesting thing is, most of the time, we know what needs to be done. We just don't want to do it because we're afraid. As discussed, people fear potential negative consequences on their performance evaluations, they fear failure, they fear being ostracized for taking a stand, etc. The potential for fear is everywhere, every day. We also know the less you fear, the more clearheaded you become. This enables you to get closer to the right conclusion and the necessary steps much faster. Fear in business slows us down. In essence, the less you fear, the better you will perform. So, how do we create a "bubble of utmost fearlessness" for ourselves, our people, and our company—especially during an implementation phase? Prepare yourself and your team not only with the best possible plan, tools, and training but also with the mindset that things will go wrong but you can all work together to overcome the roadblocks if you stay calm and focused. Let your people know you understand that when the heat is on, everything can change in a second—and you've got their backs when that happens. Tell them: "When things go right it's them; when things go unintentionally wrong, it's on you!"

## Don't Be Afraid to Pivot

Whenever you are trying to achieve big things, you will encounter resistance. That's a given. Sometimes that resistance is fierce, and no matter what you do, nothing helps. You are stuck. So, what are you going to do? Push harder? Never give up? No! Those efforts are futile when the resistance is profound. It's time to pivot. Here's an example of what that looked like in my career: My team and I were up against some very tough political dynamics in the company that prevented us from implementing a big cost-saving initiative across the entire company. What did we do? We decided to redefine success and implement the initiative first across two departments out of four, learn from the positives and negatives, and present our findings to management. Then, we hoped, they would be ready to roll out the program across all departments in an upgraded version of the original. There were a few upsides resulting from this approach. First, we were able to speed up our implementation because the resistant departments were temporarily excluded, and the other two departments were fully aligned and shared a common goal. Second, the resistant departments were "kept close" because they wanted to observe what was happening in the other two departments as they went through the implementation. Third, once the two departments reported a successful outcome to management, management itself would get the two other departments to implement and we wouldn't have to deal with their resistance anymore. Sweet! Though it took a little longer than planned, our pivot paid off big-time. The project was seen by management as a best practice and was submitted for an international award. From our perspective, it was a success—not exactly in the terms that we'd originally defined, but despite significant resistance. With our decision to pivot, we redefined the objective, implemented something positive in a difficult environment, and worked *around* the resistance rather banging our heads against it for too long. We made the best of a bad situation and ultimately achieved the goal. In my mind, that's a win! We were adaptable and did not make ourselves a target for those who resisted. The truth is an all-or-nothing approach in the face of strong resistance rarely makes sense or works. As long as you stay as close as possible to your target and do not deviate from the main strategic goal, we can call it mission accomplished.

*Leaders start building the foundation for a high-performance implementation culture well before a team needs to implement. It's an ongoing effort that must be baked into the DNA of hiring, onboarding, training, and mentoring top talent. There must be trust and alignment before implementation begins so that everyone understands their role and how the effectiveness of the implementation will be measured or adjusted according to what selected data sources tell the team. This foundation can't be built on the fly while you're executing. Once the implementation begins, your role as a leader expands. Now, you get to build on the strong foundation you've built and support your high-performance implementation culture with the set of strategies and tactics we've outlined in this chapter. The strength of the foundation you've built will be tested during every implementation—this I know for sure. How you and your team respond to those tests will offer opportunities to learn, build trust, and improve.*

# Conclusion

We've come a long way, and unsurprisingly, we've also come full circle. Our journey started with people, and now here at the end, we're talking about people again. This should be no surprise. An organization's ability to achieve great things all comes down to its people. That's why leading a business means leading the people who do the business.

In the "On People" section, we explored what it looks like to face yourself in the mirror, do an honest self-assessment of your own character traits and evolutionary biases, and improve how you lead yourself both personally and professionally. Self-awareness provides a strong foundation to become the effective and respected leader you desire to be. We also learned that organizational leadership always means leading human behavior in a group setting, where everyone is juggling their need to maximize individual benefits and collaborate. Remember, evolution has taught us that we have a better chance of surviving and thriving as individuals if we work together. This delicate interplay between the individual and the group—along with the group dynamics and behaviors this interplay encourages—is what shapes corporate culture. It's a fascinating, complicated, and necessary juggling act that we watch play out at the office every day. That's why the most powerful differentiator in the business world is a *winning culture that understands this evolutionary push and pull. But unlike the services or products we sell, it is impossible to replicate, steal, or copy a successful culture. It's something that either becomes baked into the DNA of a company or does not. We also talked about how to build teams and create a safe environment for the people on those teams. Learning to build an environment in which everyone can be as fearless as possible within established power hierarchies is the key to innovation, successful execution, and strong growth. We know that humans will not sacrifice themselves for the good of others, so establishing a winning culture requires leaders to create a culture where group members can align their individual goals with those of the team, department, or business. When leaders achieve this, they build an environment in which everyone can be intrinsically motivated to contribute to the group in order to achieve their full potential as individuals. This is when greatness happens in business, and this is why this book begins and ends with people.*

*In section two of the book, "On Strategy," we explored a meaningful definition of this often overcomplicated and misunderstood term. Strategy is how you manage today in light of your business's tomorrow to ensure continued growth through ever-changing markets and times. This, we discussed, can only happen through continuous, incremental transformation. Continuous and forward-looking change—which is something Homo sapiens avoid as much as possible, as evolution has taught us to not fix what's not broken unless absolutely necessary—will always feel difficult and uncomfortable for your people. But change is necessary for business success, so to address this evolutionary mismatch, we explored my Dynamic Stability Framework, which is designed to inform the decision-making process around strategy. No one in business school teaches us how to deal with the complex dynamics that come into play around developing business strategies, which since the beginning of mankind have never been anything other than the manifestation of the human behavior of the individuals who developed them. It's important to always keep that perspective in mind, as simply being human has the potential to derail the best intentions, amazing abilities, and great ideas. Humans like shortcuts, can get greedy, have the tendency to take out more than they are prepared to put in, can be afraid when they should be bold, can be too bold when they should be careful, can overestimate themselves, try to dominate others, etc. That's why strategy is also really about people, and the Dynamic Stability Framework is just that—a framework to navigate the learning curve.*

*Finally, we moved to the "On Implementation" section, which explores the biggest challenge of all. Nothing else really counts if a company can't implement its strategies. It's where the rubber hits the road, the gloves come off, the engines roar in anger, and you must show what you're made of as a leader. We discussed the importance of nurturing a culture of implementation excellence and that this culture must be built before and between implementations, not during them. The distinct and brilliant mix of characteristics that define this culture are a sense of urgency, fearlessness, relentless discipline, agility, resilience, and a laser focus on the desired goal, because when we lose, we take it personally. The race, as we discussed, is really won on the practice field, where relentless preparation empowers the implementation team with the skills they need to dodge the inevitable punches that implementations always bring. As the leader of a team of implementation experts, you'll have to call upon all your hard and soft skills while making sure your team feels supported, valued, and incentivized to give it their all. If you can do this, you will help your teams help your company successfully achieve continuous strategic transformation and growth through ever-changing markets and times—and this is the ultimate goal of the great leader who knows how to address the mammoth in the room!*

# Acknowledgments

This book did not "jump out of the pen." It took way too long—thirty years, to be precise. It started in the neurophysiological department of the old and famous halls of Karl–Franzens University, Graz, Austria, where, during a master's degree in neurobiology, my curiosity about human behavior awakened. The human brain, surely the single most fascinating biological structure on this planet—and in all fairness, within our entire universe, as we don't know anyone else (yet)—is where everything originates. Everything happening on this planet today is influenced by what this organ creates, produces, and results in: human behavior. Beautiful, sophisticated, complex, ununder-standable, terrible, gruesome, good, bad, ugly—it's all wired to ensure we survive as individuals and maximize the stake of our own genes in the gene pool of the next generation. After finishing my master's degree, there were more questions than answers, and the curiosity and passion to know more continued into a PhD program to understand more about the evolution of hominins in general, and us as *Homo sapiens* in particular. The most important question is how on earth can we keep up in our evolutionary time frames with the exponentially increasing speed of human society's development? I started this journey not having a mobile phone available. My chil-dren save their work on the computer by pressing the button they learned to press but don't understand. "What the heck is a floppy disk, Dad?" Even during most of the work on this book, artificial intelligence (AI) was not a thing, and only a few nerds talked about it until they got laughed out of the room. Now the single most valuable company in the world is a company that designs industry-leading GPUs, or graphic processing units (don't ask me what those are, I'm not that smart), as AI places huge computing demands on data centers. At the time of writing these acknowledgments, the market cap of this company exploded to 3.34 trillion USD. That's three thousand three hundred and forty Million USD. A number we can compute and rationalize with that very brain but surely not internalize and emotionalize (except to say "that's an awful lot"), because during our entire evolution as hominins, which somehow started around seven million years ago in Africa according to *National Geographic*, we simply did not have to. It was enough to count from one to five and then "many." But even then, after my PhD, there were more questions, because during that time, I started to lead businesses and was hit with that very human behavior of the people in the groups I had the honor of leading. From only a few in the beginning, over some dozens to multiple hundreds through many layers. So, the next question was, how does that work in companies and in businesses? I started an MBA in entre- and intrapreneurship and concentrated again on that very human behavior but specifically how it applies, develops, flourishes, blooms, crashes, destroys, and so on in the corporate world. Throughout continuous learning, making mistakes (lots of them), improving approaches, changing perspectives, looking at others, and learning how it can be done and how it can't, I was always driven by two principles. One, as one of my earliest managers taught me, you always learn the same amount when you are really trying, from the people who get it right and from the ones who get it wrong. Because in many business situations, just knowing what does *not* work is a gift and half the solution. Two, that I would never repeat anything in the way I did it once—even it was deemed as absolutely successful—because in any situation, if I could do it twice, I would know what worked perfectly and what had room for improvement, so I would be able to enhance my own and my team's performance should this situation ever occur again.

Throughout all these times, I kept writing and writing, because I felt that all these learnings might be helpful for others as well. Why should anyone have to go through all my experiences to also benefit from them? So, the idea of a book was slowly arising, and at some point, I got contacted via LinkedIn by the amazing Kathy Meis, CEO of Bublish, asking if I wanted to write a book. At that point, I already had a very nice script, although in Austrian English (which is not English at all, in fact). Unfortunately, this was the time when COVID hit, and I decided to use the time locked in and not traveling to and from work every day. The goal was to spend one hour, six days a week, on the book. I pulled that through, except that I usually went over the one-hour goal every day due to research, reading, and writing. After that year, I was ready to send the draft to Kathy. But then the real work started, as we needed to "translate" these three hundred pages of Austrian English into about one hundred fifty usable pages of American English, adapting all the Austrian and European examples, hints, jokes, and myths to the American way of communication while avoiding the many cultural, ever-evolving pitfalls. Now we're there, with a big thank-you to Kathy!

I also want and need to acknowledge many other people who helped and inspired me—knowingly or not—to raise my curiosity, increase my knowledge, and enhance my experience, all to get me over the finish line. Although I will never be able to list all of them, I want to at least call out a few. First, Heiner Roemer, my neurobiology professor at my hometown university in Graz, Austria, who was able to light the spark in me, while studying animal behavior and later focusing on human behavior, trying to understand the ununderstandable and making sense of our brain. Secondly, Michael Lehofer, philosopher, psychologist, and psychiatrist, author of many books, probably the greatest leadership coach of all time, and first and foremost my true and trusted friend for more than twenty years. Through our countless conversations, it's safe to say you influenced and taught me more than anyone else about us as humans. It's safe to say that no one knows more than you do about human behavior! Also, a big thanks to Nouchine Hadjikhani, MD, PhD, from the Athinoula A. Martinos Center for Biomedical Imaging, Associate Professor in Radiology, Harvard Medical School Director of Neurolimbic Research, for her contributions to the "Manage Power and Fear" section, where we unpack the proximate and ultimate aspects of human fear and how they impact us today in corporate settings. Then, Martin Fuchs, general manager and HR professional with the (all too rare) focus on the *human* aspect of this business function, who gave me the chance for the biggest step of my career, trusting a district sales manager in charge of eight people to become head of sales in charge of around eighty people—and then showing me the ropes in this mighty endeavor. I will always be grateful to you for this opportunity. In addition, not to forget Benoit Quittre – aka "The Boss". You taught me what business management really is about. Until I met you, I was merely practicing management on an indoor Go Kart track. You took me to Spa-Francorchamps. Along the same lines, I also need to call out Urban Skog, general manager and business executive, from whom I learned personally more than anyone else in how to truly lead versus just to manage a business. Your words are still resonating in my ear from when I had the honor to start working with you: "Nicolas, this job is too big for you, but we believe in your potential." I also need to call out Elmar Fleck, business executive and leadership coach in his own rights, for helping to pull the strings for my first international career move, which included so much more than just finding an international role, because you had to deal with not only moving an employee across the Atlantic but an entire family of six plus a dog. I will always be grateful to you for the countless hours and passion you put into making this happen. In addition, I need to mention the best team I was ever able to work with, and while it's impossible to list all the contributions you have accomplished and the brilliant expertise you are representing, I want to at least acknowledge you by listing your names (somehow in geographical order from west to east to not give any reason for revamping competition, but starting ladies first): Gabi Stich, Toni Luchner (who also wrote the foreword to this book, as he took over this amazing team once I moved on), Christoph Huebner, Fredl Lang, Florian Lambert, Franz Gfoellner, Thomas Obermeier, Philipp Wied, Christoph Miksch Aichenegg, and Christian Kellner. Together, we built the best team I was ever allowed to be part of, and I learned from our interactions more than any time before or after how to put leadership theories on the ground. Thank you all for your trust!

Finally, none of this could have been completed without my family. Thank you, my amazing wife, Madeleine, for putting up with me for thirty+ years, for managing my life throughout the professional endeavors that led our big family through so many countries and companies. For being not only okay with but also excited about the fact that when we had settled as family, when the kids were finally comfortable in schools and had again built up their friend circles, and when we finally had unpacked all boxes, the next adventure came up and we packed everything again to move on (including the additional animals we picked up at every move) to new frontiers, new countries, new companies, and new cultures. I am the luckiest husband in the world, and I thank you with all my heart, as I am so grateful to be allowed to spend my life with you! Last but not least, a super big thanks to our four spectacular kids, Rafael, Elisa, Valerie, and Isabelle. You guys are simply amazing, you rock like there is no tomorrow, you are successful in your own rights in achieving what you want to achieve in your life. Mom and Dad could not be happier, including due to the fact that you also got the globe-trotter bug, are already spread around the world and will continue to do so, and call not one country but planet Earth your home. Not even the sky is your limit! ONWARDS -"To boldly go where no one has gone before!"

# About the Author

Nicolas Pokorny is the Founder and CEO of Mammoth Leadership Sciences. He earned an MSc in Neurobiology and wrote his doctorate and master thesis for his PhD and MBA on neuroethology and the neuroscientific aspects of human behavior in group settings. He's been an entre- and intrapreneurial global marketing and sales business executive since the early 1990s specializing in building cultures of collaboration and fearlessness that drive profitability through increased engagement and continuous transformation.

His talent for developing global visions and strategies and translating them into executable plans, a fierce commitment to operational excellence, and a passion for empowering people has helped Nicolas boldly shape the future of organizations. A decisive, intelligent risk-taker, he challenges paradigms by "doing the right things rather than doing things right."

Equipped with business acumen developed over more than thirty years, his approach to apply a business framework of dynamic stability has helped businesses in mature and emerging markets to secure and optimize the basics that pay the rent today and focus on continuous innovation and transformation to execute on strategies that deliver the extraordinary results needed to navigate companies successfully through ever-changing markets and times. His track record includes multiplying global and local commercial portfolios, launching award-winning innovative business models, focusing businesses on staying lean and nimble to be able to invest in their future, and reaching all-time-high market shares.

With his keen understanding of human behavior, Nicolas has built high-performing, cross-functional, and multicultural teams. His belief that leaders must focus on the individuals first and then harness the power of the group second has helped drive transformational culture change. His approaches to talent development, team-based selling, and empowering high-performance teams have led to increases in productivity and exemplary engagement rates among the markets and teams he led.

He has lived and worked in multiple countries and companies and is still leading teams of all sizes across geographies and functions. He is an avid skier, an accomplished tennis player, a lifetime MMA athlete, with several marathons and an Iron Man under his belt. Originally from Austria, he currently resides in Massachusetts, USA, with his amazing wife, watching their four spectacular globetrotting children.

# Endnotes

1     Joshua J. Mark, "Lao-Tzu," *World History Encyclopedia*, July 9, 2020, **https://www.worldhistory.org/Lao-Tzu/**.

2     Charlotte Nickerson, "Herzberg's Two-Factor Theory Of Motivation-Hygiene," *Simply Psychology*, updated September 28, 2023, **https://www.simplypsychology.org/herzbergs-two-factor-theory.html.**

3     Carolyn Dewar and Reed Doucette, "Culture: 4 Keys to Why It Matters," *McKinsey & Company*, March 27, 2018, **https://www.mckinsey.com/capabilities/people-and-organizational-performance/our-insights/the-organization-blog/culture-4-keys-to-why-it-matters**.

4     Alison Beard, Dan McGinn, and Alicia Tillman, "Workplace Culture Conflicts," August 08, 2019, in *Dear HBR:*, produced by *Harvard Business Review*, podcast, **https://hbr.org/podcast/2019/08/workplace-culture-conflicts#**

5     Kate Heinz, "42 Shocking Company Culture Statistics You Need to Know," *Built In*, October 2, 2019, **https://builtin.com/company-culture/company-culture-statistics**.

6     Peter Herbek, *Strategische Unternehmensfuehrung: Kernkompetenzen, Identitaet und Visionen, Umsetzung, Fallbeispiele*, (Wien/Frankfurt: Wirtschaftsverlag Ueberreuter, 2000).

7     John Alcock, *Animal Behavior: An Evolutionary Approach*, 9th ed. (Sunderland, MA: Sinauer Associates, 2009).

8     Nikolaas Tinbergen, "On the Aims and Methods of Ethology," *Zeitschrift für Tierpsychologie* 20 (1963): 410-433.

9     P.W. Sherman, "The Level of Analysis," *Animal Behavior* 36 (1988): 616-618.

10    E.P. Hollander, "The Essential Interdependence of Leadership and Followership," *Current Directions in Psychological Science* 1 (1992): 71-75.

11    Mark Van Vugt, Robert Hogan, and Robert B. Kaiser, "Leadership, Followership, and Evolution: Some Lessons from the Past," *American Psychologist* 63 (2008): 182-196.

12    Andrew J. King, Dominic D. P. Johnson, Mark Van Vugt, "The Origins and Evolution of Leadership," Current Biology (2009): 19, R911–R916, **https://www.cell.com/current-biology/fulltext/S0960-9822(09)01412-2**.

13    The Origin of Species was enclosed in a letter Charles Darwin sent to Charles Lyell on 28 March 1859. The text reads: "An abstract of an Essay on the Origin of Species and Varieties Through Natural Selection by Charles Darwin M. A Fellow of the Royal, Geological & Linn. Socy. London & & & & 1859." John van Wyhe, ed., *The Complete Work of Charles Darwin Online* (2002-), accessed July 31, 2024, **https://darwin-online.org.uk/**.

14    V.C. Wynne-Edwards, *Animal Dispersion in Relation to Social Behavior* (Edinburgh: Oliver & Boyd, 1962).

15    G.C. Williams, *Adaptation and Natural Selection: A Critique of Some Current Evolutionary Thought* (Princeton, NJ: Princeton University Press, 1966).

16    T. Inagaki and N. Eisenberger, "The Neurobiology of Giving Versus Receiving Support: The Role of Stress-Related and Social Reward-Related Neural Activity," *Psychosomatic Medicine: Journal of Biobehavioral Medicine* 78 (2016).

17    Ernst Fehr, Urs Fischbacher, and Simon Gächter, "Strong reciprocity, human cooperation, and the enforcement of social norms," *Human Nature* 13 (2002): 1-25, **https://doi.org/10.1007/s12110-002-1012-7**.

18    Ernst Fehr and Klaus M. Schmidt, "Theories of Fairness and Reciprocity - Evidence and Economic Applications," December 23, 2000, **https://ssrn.com/abstract=255223**.

19     Adam Hayes, "Game Theory: A Comprehensive Guide," *Investopedia*, updated June 27, 2024, **https://www.investopedia.com/terms/g/gametheory.asp**.

20    R. Kumar, "An Introduction to Game Theory," *Irish Interdisciplinary Journal of Science & Research (IIJSR)* 8, no. 1 (January-March 2024): 1-7.

21    John von Neumann and Oskar Morgenstern, *Theory of Games and Economic Behavior: 60th Anniversary Commemorative Edition* (Princeton, NJ: Princeton University Press, 2004), **https://press.princeton.edu/books/paperback/9780691130613/theory-of-games-and-economic-behavior**.

22    "John F. Nash Jr. – Facts," NobelPrize.org, last modified 2024, **https://www.nobelprize.org/prizes/economic-sciences/1994/nash/facts/**.

23    John F. Nash, "The Bargaining Problem," *Econometrica* 18, no. 2 (1950): 155-162.

24     David M. Kreps, "Nash Equilibrium," in *Game Theory*, ed. John Eatwell, Murray Milgate, and Peter Newman, The New Palgrave (London: Palgrave Macmillan, 1989), **https://doi.org/10.1007/978-1-349-20181-5_19**.

25     *A Beautiful Mind*, directed by Ron Howard, (United States: Universal Pictures, 2001).

26     Jonathan Bendor and Piotr Swistak, "The Evolution of Norms," *American Journal of Sociology* 106, no. 6 (2001): 1493-1545.

27     Ernst Fehr and Klaus M. Schmidt, "A Theory of Fairness, Competition, and Cooperation," *The Quarterly Journal of Economics* 114, no. 3 (1999): 817-868.

28     Ernst Fehr, Georg Kirchsteiger, and Arno Riedl, "Does Fairness Prevent Market Clearing? An Experimental Investigation," *The Quarterly Journal of Economics* 108, no. 2 (May 1993): 437-459, **https://doi.org/10.2307/2118338**.

29     Colin F. Camerer and Ernst Fehr, "When Does 'Economic Man' Dominate Social Behavior?" *Science* 311 (2006): 47-52, **https://doi.org/10.1126/science.1110600**.

30     Joyce Berg, John Dickhaut, and Kevin McCabe, "Trust, Reciprocity, and Social History," *Games and Economic Behavior* 10, no. 1 (1995): 122-142, **https://doi.org/10.1006/game.1995.1027**.

31     Nahoko Hayashi, Elinor Ostrom, James Walker, and Toshio Yamagishi, "Reciprocity, Trust, and the Sense of Control: A Cross-Societal Study," *Rationality and Society* 11, no. 1 (1999): 27-46.

32     Doug Metzger, *Literature and History*, podcast, **https://literatureandhistory.com/index.php?option=com_content&view=article&id=250&catid=2**.

33    Samuel Johnson, *The Vanity of Human Wishes: The Tenth Satire of Juvenal, Imitated,* **https://www.poetryfoundation. org/poems/44448/the-vanity-of-human-wishes**.

34    Mark T. Ford, Chris P. Cerasoli, Jennifer A. Higgins, and Andrew L. DeCesare, "Relationships Between Psychological, Physical, and Behavioral Health and Work Performance: A Review and Meta-Analysis," *Work & Stress* 25, no. 3 (2011): 185-204, **https://doi.org/10.1080/02678373.2011.609035**.

35    Simon Sinek, *Leaders Eat Last* (New York: Portfolio, 2014).

36    Henry Cloud, Boundaries for Leaders, (New York: HarperCollins, 2013).

37    Paul J. Zak, "The Neuroscience of Trust," *Harvard Business Review,* (January–February 2017), **https://hbr.org/2017/01/ the-neuroscience-of-trust**

38    "Power," Open Education Sociology Dictionary, accessed July 31, 2024, **https://sociologydictionary.org/power/**.

39    John R.P. French and Bertram Raven, "The Bases of Social Power," in *Studies in Social Power,* ed. Dorwin Cartwright (Ann Arbor, MI: Institute for Social Research, 1959), 150-167.

40    Dorwin Cartwright, ed., *Studies in Social Power* (Ann Arbor, MI: University of Michigan, 1959), 150-167.

41    Takeshi Furuichi, *Bonobo and Chimpanzee: The Lessons of Social Coexistence,* 1st ed., Primatology Monographs (Cham: Springer, 2019).

42    Robert M. Sapolsky, *Why Zebras Don't Get Ulcers: The Acclaimed Guide to Stress, Stress-Related Diseases, and Coping,* 3rd ed. (New York: Henry Holt, 2004).

43    Renee D. Goodwin, Andrea H. Weinberger, June H. Kim, Melody Wu, Sandro Galea, "Trends in Anxiety Among Adults in the United States, 2008-2018: Rapid Increases Among Young Adults," *Journal of Psychiatry Research* 130 (November 2020): 411-446, **https://doi.org/10.1016/j.jpsychires.2020.08.014**.

44    American Psychological Association, *Stress in America: The State of Our Nation*, Stress in America™ Survey (2017), **https://www.stressinamerica.org**.

45    Thom Mayer, *Battling Healthcare Burnout: Learning to Love the Job You Have, While Creating the Job You Love* (Oakland, CA: Berrett-Koehler Publishers, 2021).

46    Michael P. Leiter and Wilmar B. Schaufeli, "Consistency of the Burnout Construct Across Occupations," *Anxiety, Stress, and Coping* 9, no. 3 (1996): 229-243.

47    "Stress," World Health Organization, accessed July 31, 2024, **https://www.who.int/news-room/questions-and-answers/item/stress**.

48    "Anxiety," American Psychological Association, accessed July 31, 2024, **https://www.apa.org/topics/anxiety**.

49    "Any Anxiety Disorder," National Institute of Mental Health, accessed July 31, 2024, **https://www.nimh.nih.gov/health/statistics/any-anxiety-disorder**.

50    Garen Staglin, "Stress Management for Leaders, Improved Mental Health for the Workplace," *Forbes*, April 25, 2023, **https://www.forbes.com/sites/onemind/2023/04/25/stress-management-for-leaders-improved-mental-health-for-the-workplace/**

51    Beatrice de Gelder, Josh Snyder, Doug Greve, George
      Gerard, and Nouchine Hadjikhani, "Fear Fosters Flight: A
      Mechanism for Fear Contagion When Perceiving Emotion
      Expressed by a Whole Body," *Proceedings of the National
      Academy of Sciences* 101, no. 47 (2004): 16701-16706.

52    Albert Mehrabian, *Silent Messages: Implicit Communication
      of Emotions and Attitudes*, 2nd ed. (Belmont, CA: Wadsworth,
      1981).

53    Antoine de Saint-Exupéry, *Le Petit Prince* (Stuttgart: Klett,
      1986).

54    Sun Tzu, *The Art of War*, trans. Lionel Giles (Bridgewater, MA:
      World Publications, 2007).

55    Tera Allas and Bill Schaninger, "The boss factor: Making
      the world a better place through workplace relationships,"
      McKinsey & Company, September 22, 2020, **https://www.
      mckinsey.com/capabilities/people-and-organizational-
      performance/our-insights/the-boss-factor-making-the-
      world-a-better-place-through-workplace-relationships#/**

56    Spencer Johnson, *Who Moved My Cheese?* (London:
      Vermilion, 2001).

57    Mark Van Vugt and Richard Ronay, "The Evolutionary
      Psychology of Leadership: Theory, Review, and Roadmap,"
      *Organizational Psychology Review* 4, no. 1 (2014): 74-95.

58    Leda Cosmides and John Tooby, *Evolutionary Psychology: A
      Primer*, Vol. 13 (Santa Barbara, CA: Center for Evolutionary
      Psychology, 1997).

59    "Walmart Inc. (WMT) Company Profile," *Yahoo Finance*,
      accessed July 31, 2024, **https://finance.yahoo.com/quote/
      WMT/profile/?p=WMT**.

60      Robert S. Kaplan and David P. Norton, "The Office of Strategy Management," *Harvard Business Review*, October 2005, **https://hbr.org/2005/10/the-office-of-strategy-management.**

61      Joyce Hogan, Robert Hogan, and Robert B. Kaiser, "Management Derailment," in *American Psychological Association Handbook of Industrial and Organizational Psychology*, ed. Sheldon Zedeck, vol. 3 (Washington, DC: American Psychological Association, 2010), 555-575.

62      Martie G. Haselton and David M. Buss, "Error Management Theory: A New Perspective on Biases in Cross-Sex Mind Reading," *Journal of Personality and Social Psychology* 78 (2000): 81.

63      Martie G. Haselton and Daniel Nettle, "The Paranoid Optimist: An Integrative Evolutionary Model of Cognitive Biases," *Personality and Social Psychology Review* 10 (2006): 47–66.

64      Laura Betzig, "Sex, Succession, and Stratification in the First Six Civilizations: How Powerful Men Reproduced, Passed Power on to Their Sons, and Used Power to Defend Their Wealth, Women, and Children," in *Social Stratification and Socioeconomic Inequality*, vol. 1, ed. Lee Ellis (Westport, CT: Praeger, 1993), 37-74.

65      Art Padilla, Robert Hogan, and Robert B. Kaiser, "The Toxic Triangle: Destructive Leaders, Vulnerable Followers, and Conducive Environments," *Leadership Quarterly* 18 (2007): 176-194.

66      John Kotter, "Barriers to Change: The Real Reason Behind the Kodak Downfall," *Forbes*, May 2, 2012, **https://www.forbes.com/sites/johnkotter/2012/05/02/barriers-to-change-the-real-reason-behind-the-kodak-downfall/**

67 Yves L. Doz, "The Strategic Decisions That Caused Nokia's Failure," *INSEAD*, November 23, 2017, **https://knowledge.insead.edu/strategy/strategic-decisions-caused-nokias-failure**.

68 Peterson, M. (2017). An introduction to decision theory. Cambridge University Press.

69 Michael E. Porter, "What Is Strategy?" *Harvard Business Review*, November–December 1996, **https://hbr.org/1996/11/what-is-strategy**

70 "Jeep® Brand Reveals Plan for Global Leadership in SUV Electrification," Stellantis, September 8, 2022, **https://www.media.stellantis.com/em-en/jeep/press/jeep-brand-reveals-plan-for-global-leadership-in-suv-electrification**

71 "What Is a Recession?" *McKinsey & Company*, updated July 11, 2024, **https://www.mckinsey.com/featured-insights/mckinsey-explainers/what-is-a-recession**.

72 Will Douglas Heaven, "Why Meta's latest large language model survived only three days online," *MIT Technology Review*, November 18, 2022, **https://www.technologyreview.com/2022/11/18/1063487/meta-large-language-model-ai-only-survived-three-days-gpt-3-science/**.

73 "Growing beyond the core business," *McKinsey & Company*, July 1, 2015, **https://www.mckinsey.com/capabilities/strategy-and-corporate-finance/our-insights/growing-beyond-the-core-business**.

74 Jerome H. Barkow, Leda Cosmides, and John Tooby, *The Adapted Mind: Evolutionary Psychology and the Generation of Culture* (New York: Oxford University Press, 1992).

75 David M. Buss, ed., *Handbook of Evolutionary Psychology* (Hoboken, NJ: Wiley, 2005).

76   Mark Schaller, Jeffry A. Simpson, and Douglas T. Kenrick, eds., *Evolution and Social Psychology* (New York: Psychology Press, 2006).

77   Martie G. Haselton and David M. Buss, "Error Management Theory: A New Perspective on Biases in Cross-Sex Mind Reading," *Journal of Personality and Social Psychology* 78 (2000): 78, 81.

78   Martie G. Haselton and Daniel Nettle, "The Paranoid Optimist: An Integrative Evolutionary Model of Cognitive Biases," *Personality and Social Psychology Review* 10 (2006): 47–66.

79   Laurie R. Santos and Alexandra G. Rosati, "The Evolutionary Roots of Human Decision Making," *Annual Review of Psychology* 66, no. 1 (2015): 321-347.

80   Associated Press, "WeWork Has Emerged from Bankruptcy. What's Next for the Co-Working Office Space Provider?" *U.S. News & World Report*, June 12, 2024, **https://www.usnews.com/news/business/articles/2024-06-12/wework-has-emerged-from-bankruptcy-whats-next-for-the-co-working-office-space-provider**

81   Russell Hotten, "Volkswagen: The scandal explained," *BBC News*, December 10, 2015, **https://www.bbc.com/news/business-34324772.**

82   Program On Negotiation Staff, "Deal-Making Don'ts: Lessons from Yahoo's Tumblr Acquisition," Harvard Law School, December 5, 2023, **https://www.pon.harvard.edu/daily/business-negotiations/yahoos-tumblr-acquisition-nb/**

83   Joyce Hogan, Robert Hogan, and Robert B. Kaiser, "Management Derailment," in *American Psychological Association Handbook of Industrial and Organizational Psychology*, ed. Sheldon Zedeck, vol. 3 (Washington, DC: American Psychological Association, 2010), 555-575.

84    Gordon Tredgold, "**The One Mistake Many Leaders Make That Disengages Their Staff**," *Inc.*, January 23, 2018, **https://www.inc.com/gordon-tredgold/the-challenge-of-working-for-a-know-it-all-boss.html**

85    Robin I. M. Dunbar, *Grooming, Gossip, and the Evolution of Language* (London: Faber & Faber, 2004).

86    Robert A. Foley, "The Adaptive Legacy of Human Evolution: A Search for the Environment of Evolutionary Adaptedness," *Evolutionary Anthropology* 4 (1997): 194–203.

87    Mark Van Vugt and Paul A. M. Van Lange, "The Altruism Puzzle: Psychological Adaptations for Prosocial Behaviour," in *Evolution and Social Psychology*, ed. Mark Schaller, Douglas T. Kenrick, and Jeffry A. Simpson (New York: Psychology Press, 2006), 237–261.

88    "Two-Pizza Teams," in *Introduction to DevOps on AWS*, Amazon Web Services, accessed July 31, 2024, **https://docs.aws.amazon.com/whitepapers/latest/introduction-devops-aws/two-pizza-teams.html**.

89    Statista. **https://www.statista.com/statistics/261463/ceo-to-worker-compensation-ratio-of-top-firms-in-the-us/#:~:text=In%202022%2C%20it%20was%20estimated,key%20industry%20of%20their%20firm**.

90    Mark Van Vugt, "The Evolutionary Origins of Leadership and Followership," *Personality and Social Psychology Review* 10 (2006): 354–372.

91    Anton Barbashin. **https://www.cnbc.com/2022/03/31/russias-putin-is-so-powerful-everyone-is-scared-to-tell-him-the-truth.html**

92    "Bonobo," World Wildlife Fund, accessed July 31, 2024, **https://www.worldwildlife.org/species/bonobo**.

93     Mark Van Vugt and Tatsuya Kameda, "Evolution and Groups," in *Group Processes*, ed. John Levine (New York: Psychology Press, 2012), 297–322.

94     Stephen R. Covey, *The 8th Habit: From Effectiveness to Greatness*, (New York: Free Press, Chicago, 2004).

95     "UK-Based F1 Teams Unite Around 'Project Pitlane' to Assist with Ventilator Production," *Formula 1*, accessed July 31, 2024, **https://www.formula1.com/en/latest/article/uk-based-f1-teams-unite-around-project-pitlane-to-assist-with-ventilator.7G8gQu9v8j6aSgqk3P52fp**.